Physical Education for Homeschool, Classroom, and Recreation Settings

102 Games With Variations

John Byl
and
Bettie VanGils Kloet

D1474128

Human Kinetics

Library of Congress Cataloging-in-Publication Data

Byl, John.
 Physical education for homeschool, classroom, and recreation settings : 102 games with variations / John Byl, Bettie VanGils Kloet.
   pages cm
 Includes bibliographical references.
 1. Physical education for children--Study and teaching--Activity programs. 2. Physical education for children--Curricula. 3. Home schooling. I. Kloet, Bettie VanGils. II. Title.
 GV443.B95 2014
 372.86044--dc23
                                2013031973
 ISBN-10: 1-4504-6777-6 (print)
 ISBN-13: 978-1-4504-6777-3 (print)

Copyright © 2014 by John Byl and Bettie VanGils Kloet

The web addresses cited in this text were current as of February 7, 2014, unless otherwise noted.

Acquisitions Editor: Diana Vincer; **Developmental Editor:** Melissa Feld; **Assistant Editors:** Kevin Matz and Rachel Fowler; **Copyeditor:** Patricia L. MacDonald; **Proofreader:** Anne Rumery; **Permissions Manager:** Dalene Reeder; **Graphic Designer:** Dawn Sills; **Cover Designer:** Keith Blomberg; **Photographs (cover):** Photodisc; **Photographs (interior):** John Byl; **Photo Asset Manager:** Laura Fitch; **Visual Production Assistant:** Joyce Brumfield; **Photo Production Manager:** Jason Allen; **Art Manager:** Kelly Hendren; **Associate Art Manager:** Alan L. Wilborn; **Illustrations:** © Human Kinetics; **Printer:** United Graphics

Printed in the United States of America   10   9   8   7   6   5   4   3   2   1

The paper in this book is certified under a sustainable forestry program.

Human Kinetics
Website: www.HumanKinetics.com

United States: Human Kinetics
P.O. Box 5076
Champaign, IL 61825-5076
800-747-4457
e-mail: humank@hkusa.com

Canada: Human Kinetics
475 Devonshire Road Unit 100
Windsor, ON N8Y 2L5
800-465-7301 (in Canada only)
e-mail: info@hkcanada.com

Europe: Human Kinetics
107 Bradford Road
Stanningley
Leeds LS28 6AT, United Kingdom
+44 (0) 113 255 5665
e-mail: hk@hkeurope.com

Australia: Human Kinetics
57A Price Avenue
Lower Mitcham, South Australia 5062
08 8372 0999
e-mail: info@hkaustralia.com

New Zealand: Human Kinetics
P.O. Box 80
Torrens Park, South Australia 5062
0800 222 062
e-mail: info@hknewzealand.com

E6105

CONTENTS

GAME FINDER

The games in the game finder are listed alphabetically to make them easier to locate. The icons indicate that a game is especially well suited to that activity or that the activity could use specific equipment. Some of the activities, such as the warm-up and fitness activities, could be used for other sports as well as a general warm-up or fitness activity but do not require a specific ball or other equipment. To find a particular game which fits into the Teaching Games for Understanding approach, locate the category in the top row and then look in that column to find the game you want.

Key

Warm-Up		Football	
Dance		Lacrosse	
Gymnastics		Hockey	
Target		Badminton	
Soccer		Tennis	
Basketball		Volleyball	
Disc		Baseball or softball	

Game	Page	Warm-up	Dance	Gym-nastics	Target	Invasion						Net			Strike
Aerobic Routine	194		●												
Alligators	64	●													
Balance Race	138											●			
Balancing Bodies	211			●											
Baseball Without Baserunning	153														●
Beanbag Toss to Partner	142													●	
Bench Push-Ups and Triceps Dips	65	●													
Bench Step-Ups	27	●													
Body Parts	28	●													
Card Bouncers	105					●	●				●			●	
Catch What You Can	169									●					
Cone Square	30	●													
Cumbia Urbana	196		●												
Dance Cards for Line Dancing	189		●												
Disc Archery	74					●		●			●		●		
Disc Golf	76	●			●	●		●	●	●	●		●	●	●
Double Cone Ball	125					●				●	●				
Double Disc Court	78					●		●	●	●			●		

(continued)

vii

(continued)

Game	Page	Warm-up	Dance	Gym-nastics	Target	Invasion						Net		Strike
Grid Pass	121					soccer	basketball	frisbee	football	lacrosse	hockey			
He Shoots, He Scores	89				bowling	soccer								
Hit It Down or Intercept	131							frisbee	football					
Hog	108					soccer	basketball			lacrosse	hockey			
Hopscotch Potsy	90				bowling									
Hot Box	179													baseball
Hut	102	heart							football					
In-the-Ballpark Home Runs	46	heart				soccer	basketball			lacrosse	hockey			baseball
Jugglers	119					soccer								
Jump Rope	47	heart												
Kangaroos and Penguins	49	heart												
Ladders	51	heart												
Long Accuracy Rolls	83				bowling	soccer								
Long Accuracy Throws	92					soccer	basketball	frisbee	football	lacrosse	hockey			baseball
Long Trap	173					soccer	basketball	frisbee	football	lacrosse	hockey	shuttlecock	volleyball	baseball
Medicine Ball Pass	67	heart												
Mini Volleyball	145												volleyball	
Mirror	132					soccer	basketball	frisbee	football	lacrosse	hockey			
Miss the Pins	84				bowling									

Game	Page	Warm-up	Dance	Gymnastics	Target	Invasion						Net			Strike
					(bowling)	(soccer)	(basketball)	(frisbee)	(football)	(lacrosse)	(hockey)	(badminton)	(tennis)	(volleyball)	(baseball)
Nailing It	80				●	●	●	●	●	●	●	●	●	●	●
Net Toss	146													●	
No-Defense Running	181	●													●
No-Net Consecutive Hits	140											●			●
Noodle Paddle	156														●
Obstacle Dribble	109					●	●			●	●				
Offensive Attack	127					●	●				●				
One-Goal Soccer	129					●					●				
Partner Net Toss	147													●	
Partner Pass	123					●	●	●	●	●	●				
Partner Wall Spike	149													●	
Passing Threes	53	●				●	●		●		●			●	
Passing Volleyballs	164													●	
Plank Holds	69	●													
Quick Relay Pass	166					●	●	●	●	●	●				●
Record for Distance	157						●	●	●	●					●
Record for Maximum Time Aloft	158						●	●	●	●					●
Record for Throw, Run, and Catch	174	●				●	●	●	●	●					●
Resting Volley	168													●	

(continued)

Game	Page	Warm-up	Dance	Gym-nastics	Target	Invasion						Net		Strike
Robin's Nest	111					soccer	basketball							
Rock, Paper, Scissors Chase	55	heart				soccer	basketball				hockey			
Rollers	175					soccer	basketball	frisbee	football	lacrosse				baseball
Rolling Goals	176					soccer								
Rolling Skills	206			gymnast										
Running Circles	57	heart				soccer	basketball			lacrosse	hockey			
Shuttle Run With Blocks	58	heart												
Slalom Course	113											shuttlecock	racket	
Sliders	133					soccer								baseball
Slow Dribbler	114					soccer								
Soccer Baseball	159					soccer								baseball
Soccer Billiards	93					soccer								
Speed Trap	120					soccer								
Split Triangle Run	59	heart				soccer	basketball		football		hockey	shuttlecock	volleyball	baseball
Sprinters	115	heart				soccer	basketball				hockey			
Stepper-Board Catch	177								football					baseball
Subtract a Jack	61	heart												
Tabata Drills	62	heart												
Tail Ball	63	heart												baseball

Game	Page	Warm-up	Dance	Gym-nastics	Target	Invasion						Net	Strike
Tail Tag	134	♥							🏈				
Teeing Off	161												⚾
Ten-Pin Slam	86				🎳								
Three in a Row	95												⚾
Throw for Points	162						🏀	🥏	🏈	⚹			⚾
Tight-Quarter Dribble	116					⚽	🏀				🏒		
Timed Ball Kicks	97					⚽	🏀			⚹	🏒		
Timed Wall Dribble	99	♥					🏀			⚹	🏒		
Transfer-ence of Weight	209			🤸									
Two Goal-keepers	130					⚽							
Two-to-One Keep-Away	124					⚽	🏀	🥏	🏈	⚹	🏒		
Two-Player Bowling	88				🎳								
Up and Down	71	♥											
Wall Ball	141											🏸	
Wall Spike	150											🏐	
Walling for Distance	101					⚽	🏀	🥏	🏈	⚹	🏒		⚾
What Time Is It, Mr. Wolf?	118					⚽	🏀				🏒		
X Dance	187		🩰										

PREFACE

Some of us may recall playing games in our neighborhoods with two or three other children. We modified the rules to suit our needs, we had fun, and we learned. This text brings us back to those days when children learned through games that require very little equipment, use small groups of two to four children (and maybe even a few adults), and engage players in fun learning. This book is designed with both the parent and teacher in mind—although the primary interest is helping children learn and develop through fun physical activities. The activities are ideal for homeschool parents and for parents who wish to supplement their children's physical education instruction or just have some physically active fun with their children. The ideas in this book are also great for physical education in schools, whether the teacher divides the class into smaller groups or is teaching in a small school with few students in each class. After-school programs, and other recreational, intramural, and recess programs, often have smaller groups, and these games are ideal in those settings as well. This book is about fundamental skill development and understanding games through engaging and purposeful playful activity based on the American Academy of Pediatrics' research, the Canadian Sport for Life model, and the Teaching Games for Understanding approach.

The first chapter sets the big picture by grounding this book in important research, including yearly lesson plans for grades K–5. Teaching Games for Understanding provides the structure for this book, and enhancing physical literacy is key to the activities. Equipment requirements include basic fitness and sports equipment that could be used in and around a home or at a local community park. Teaching activities usually involve game playing. The games are organized in categories and then alphabetically to make them easy to find. The game finder will also help you locate the games and see at a glance which are suitable for different sports.

Active movement, positive health, and physical fitness contribute to a positive experience of life and enhance learning. Physical education is foundational to healthy schooling. This book provides practical guidance for parents and teachers as they help children develop and maintain their physical fitness and physical activity skills. For younger children some activities may need to be simplified, while for older children some activities may need to be modified to be more challenging. Involve the children in adjusting rules to best suit their interests and needs—game rules reflect people's interests and values. Variations to games are provided, but make further adjustments to best meet the needs of your students.

Chapter 2 briefly outlines the importance and role of warming up, cooling down, and stretching and provides fun games that warm up the students' bodies and get them ready for the activities that follow. This chapter also includes engaging fitness activities to be used in each lesson. When engaging in activities, we recommend doing a warm-up activity, then a fitness activity, and then any of the other activities, followed by a cool-down. Chapters 3 through 6 provide full descriptions of all the games referred to in the lesson outlines found in chapter 1. Chapters 7 and 8 provide activities for teaching movement skills in dance and gymnastics.

The games in chapters 2 through 6 are broken down into easy-to-use components. The first is the key objectives of the game. We then identify the key skills used in the game and suggest various sports for which these games would work. Next is the recommended equipment, but remember that many games work with different equipment (e.g., many hockey games can also be played with soccer balls). The game setup and how to play the game are found in the instructions. Sometimes a game variation is provided, and you and your children are encouraged to make and explore your own variations as well. Finally, there are two or more questions for understanding. These questions help the students understand the main principles of the games they are playing and let them connect these principles with many other game situations. Although dance and gymnastics are not really games, they are important parts of a well-rounded physical education program. With the suggestions made in this book, these activities can be taught with a lot of fun and without too much difficulty.

When we think of children getting through their daily schedules, we hope that each day involves some movement and physical activity. Children with healthy bodies and sufficient physical activity (optimally 90 minutes a day) are happier and learn better than their peers who lead sedentary lives. Adults who get regular exercise (at least six times a day for 10 minutes) are better parents, teachers, and spouses. It is important that adults be positive and physically active role models. Fun activities make the time fly, the experience is desired, and the overall health of participants is improved.

We often need to think outside the box to teach sports skills to small groups of children that are more easily taught in large groups in a gymnasium, but that same thinking allows us to help our children develop lifelong exercise habits. This book provides easy-to-follow guidelines for a comprehensive, educational, challenging, and fun physical education program.

So you can keep getting helpful ideas, we have created a website as well as Facebook and Pinterest pages. Stay connected and learn at the following sites:

www.pe4homeschool.com
www.facebook.com/HomeSchoolPhysicalEducation
http://pinterest.com/homeschoolpe/boards

Enjoy life. Run with it. Let's play ball!

ACKNOWLEDGMENTS

For various sections of this book we were assisted by a number of people. For some of the football ideas, one of John's classes helped. Their names are Stuart Bender, Richard Brouwer, Justin Corvers, Brad Douwes, Joel Dykxhoorn, Lance Haverkamp, Ben Higgs, Reuben Langendoen, Breanne Martin, Matt Neal, Jessica Ramsay, Kendall Straatsma, and Jonathan Tweedle. The gymnastics section was written by Jane Sinden. For the disc ideas, Chris Lowcock from Ontario Disc Sports Association provided helpful suggestions. Some of the great ideas on the use of beanbags came from Hannah Braam.

Thank you to the many people at various conferences for their suggestions, questions, and encouragement to produce this book. The CanFitPro conference and CIRA Ontario helped us immensely as professionals in this field. We gratefully acknowledge the creative ideas stimulated by other conference speakers such as Silken Laumann and Mindy Mylrea, two truly great fitness advocates and innovative thinkers.

To the folks at Human Kinetics, thanks for stepping out on a limb to support this book. We are positive the limb is strong enough and your faith in us will be rewarded. Particularly to Jake Rondot and Scott Wikgren, thanks for your invaluable support and perceptive comments as we developed the concept of this book. Thank you to John's student worker, Sarah Eerkes, for helping him out with many things, including some initial editing.

Our deep appreciation is offered to some homeschooled children who have been marvelous guinea pigs. A special thanks to Aaron, Matthew, Soren, Rosie, Hunter, Sidney, Abby, Kenneth, Matthew, and Sarah, who helped with a test run of the entire curriculum.

As coauthors, we want to thank each other for the way we wrote this book together. We contributed equally, and John could assist Bettie as a first-time author, and Bettie could assist John as one newer to homeschooling.

From Bettie: Thank you Rob, Jessica, Sarah, and Matthew for being such a supportive and encouraging family. Thank you, Rob, for believing in me. I also offer my thanks to God, who has blessed me with energy, health, and His boundless love. From John: I echo Bettie's comments and in particular want to thank my wife, Catherine, for her incredible support and love, and, because of my writing, often having a little less of me than if I did not write.

UNDERSTANDING THE BIG PICTURE

If you don't know where you are going,
you will wind up somewhere else.

Yogi Berra

Congratulations! By beginning to read this book, you have begun your journey to a deeper understanding of and commitment to enhancing the physical activity of your small group. Some of you will divide a large group into small units so that students benefit from more active participation and learning opportunities provided by smaller groupings. *Physical Education for Homeschool, Classroom, and Recreation Settings* is grounded in the research of the American Academy of Pediatrics on the importance of play; the Canadian Sport for Life model, which uses a developmental approach to learning; physical literacy, which is about the ABCs of movement; and the Teaching Games for Understanding approach, which has students learn concepts that can be applied to many different games. This book uses games to teach skills and concepts that are fundamentally helpful for the overall development and health of your students.

Play is vitally important for the healthy development of children. The United Nations recognizes "the right of the child to rest and leisure, to engage in play and recreational activities appropriate to the age of the child" (Convention on the Rights of the Child, n.d.). The American Academy of Pediatrics (AAP) concurs. In the position paper "The Importance of Play in Promoting Healthy Child Development and Maintaining Strong Parent–Child Bonds" (2007), the AAP argues that the benefits of play include at least these three major areas:

1. Play allows children to use their creativity while developing their imagination, dexterity, and physical, cognitive, and emotional strength. Play is important to healthy brain development.

2. Children's developmental trajectory is critically mediated by appropriate, affective relationships with loving and consistent caregivers as they relate to children through play.

3. Play is integral to the academic environment. It ensures that the school setting attends to the social and emotional development of children as well as their cognitive development.

Early in children's development, well before they complete their growth spurts, it is important to develop such fundamental skills as agility, balance, coordination, and speed and to learn them in a fun way. Some sports such as gymnastics, diving, and figure skating require specialization at a young age. However, most lifelong sports are late-specialization sports, such as soccer, basketball, and volleyball. For these sports, specialization should not occur before the ages of 12 to 15. For most sports, children benefit from having well-rounded experiences in a wide variety of activities. Based on the research that formulated the Canadian Sport for Life model, this book provides a broad assortment of games helpful for enhancing the general movement abilities of the participants. For more on the Sport for Life model go to www.canadian sportforlife.ca.

To be literate in the English language one needs to learn about nouns and verbs; to be literate in mathematics one needs to learn about adding and subtracting; to be literate in physical education one needs to learn about moving, controlling objects, and balancing on different surfaces and in different environments (on the ground, in water, on snow, on ice, and in the air). Moving includes such skills as climbing, gliding, hopping, jumping, running, skating, skipping, swimming, and wheeling. Controlling objects includes sending (kicking, rolling, striking, and throwing); receiving by catching, stopping, and trapping; traveling with objects by dribbling with the feet, the hands, or sticks; and receiving and sending when striking an object like in baseball or volleyball. Balancing includes such things as center of balance, rolling, dodging, floating, landing, falling, spinning, stopping, swinging, and twisting or turning. These fundamental movement skills help participants engage with confidence in a variety of sports. For more information on physical literacy, go to www.canadiansportforlife.ca/learn-about-canadian-sport-life/physical-literacy.

TEACHING GAMES FOR UNDERSTANDING

Engaging in sports and games can be fun, and it helps players better understand games in general. Teaching Games for Understanding (TGfU) is a model developed by Bunker and Thorpe in the early 1980s (Bunker and Thorpe 1982). This model has several significant strategies and important benefits, and its use is recommended in this book. Let's look at how these strategies and benefits can be applied. Do not be intimidated by this approach; it simply engages the students in learning through asking questions about game understanding.

When baseball is no longer fun, it's no longer a game.

Joe DiMaggio

Bunker and Thorpe outlined the model as having six steps (see figure 1.1), much of which is further developed in Butler and Griffin's book *More Teaching Games for Understanding: Moving Globally* (2010).

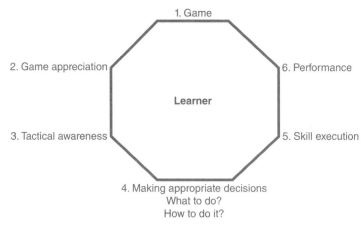

Figure 1.1 TGfU model.

"Teaching games for understanding: Evolution of a model," P. Werner, R. Thorpe, and D. Bunker, *JOPERD* 1: 129, 1966, adapted by permission of the publisher (Taylor & Francis Ltd, http://www.tandf.co.uk/journals).

• **Step 1: Keep it simple but change accordingly.** Games are taught in a simple form to small numbers of players and are therefore readily modified to suit the needs and goals of the participants—especially if the children you are teaching have varied skills. Using smaller numbers is ideal in a homeschool setting. We all know the story of Goldilocks and the three bears and how Goldilocks ate only one bowl of porridge because the other two were either too hot or too cold. If she had only put the hot one in the fridge and the cold one in the microwave, she could have enjoyed three bowls of porridge. The same can be said about the games in this book. Most are presented in a basic form, but if even that kind of game is too "hot" (i.e., too challenging for the players), help the players modify the game until it works well for them. If the game is too "cold" (i.e., too simple or lacking sufficient activity, or challenge, or excitement), encourage players to modify the game to make it work well for them. Small-sided games focus player attention more, involve more touches with the ball, and because they are less complex, make it easier for players to analyze and develop skills and strategies for improvement. Furthermore, players begin thinking strategically about game concepts while developing skills within a realistic context.

The process of making the changes students want can be quick and simple. When a student suggests a change, clarify her comment so that everyone understands, and then ask all the players to give a thumbs up if they agree with the change or a thumbs down if they disagree. If the suggested change gets a thumbs up from most players, then incorporate the change and see how it works. Thumbs up or down is a time-effective way of voting so that attention can be focused on playing the games and discussing improvements.

- **Step 2: Appreciate the playing time.** Help players gain a quick appreciation of the game. The rules in this book are simple and quick to explain so that playing and learning time is maximized and instructional and organizational time is minimized. Besides, the many games add variety and are more stimulating than out-of-context drills.

- **Step 3: Understand game tactics.** Players should understand the tactics of the game and be able to apply those to other games (i.e., the tactics and skills are transferable to other activities). Some of the key components included in this book are representative of what one finds in games such as football, soccer, rugby, and basketball. Periodic breaks in game playing should be used to help players discuss and learn tactical improvements. Games are valuable, but they become more valuable when we allow players time to reflect and answer questions of how and why. Without thinking things through, game playing may become teaching games with *no* understanding. Younger players will be able to transfer learnings to simple games; older players will be able to transfer learnings to more advanced games. This transference of learning works best in related games. In the TGfU model, the groups of games include target games such as bowling; territory and invasion games such as soccer; net and wall games such as tennis; and striking and fielding games such as baseball. Chapters 3 through 6 in this book are organized around those related games.

- **Step 4: Make real-time decisions.** Players should develop their decision-making skills in terms of what to do and how to do it. Although tactics can be developed, there is nothing like the real-life decision making that takes place instantaneously during the ebb and flow of a game. Offensively, these games deal with penetrating the defensive zone and evading detection and contact. In each game, players should take time to reflect on their personal experiences and observations of others in terms of the tactics and movements that are most effective.

A fun way for players to learn about effective offensive and defensive strategies is to assign one or two players to take turns being television announcers. These announcers can do a play-by-play description of what is happening, describing why and how a player has avoided detection or has been caught. The announcers can also do a recap describing why certain players excelled at their offensive or defensive play.

I've missed more than 9,000 shots in my career.
I've lost almost 300 games.
Twenty-six times I've been trusted to take the game-winning shot and missed.
I've failed over and over and over again in my life.
And that is why I succeed.

Michael Jordan

• **Step 5: Drills related to immediate needs.** This step concerns helping players execute their physical skills. It may be helpful after or during a game to take time to let students explore and practice such individual skills as dodging, making quick turns, or passing and catching balls. Carefully constructed and focused practices and drills should have an immediate impact on playing ability.

• **Step 6: Transfer what is learned in one game to another.** Because participants have played and worked their way through the first five steps, their performance will improve. Ideally the better performance will necessitate further modifications of the games to accommodate these improvements and challenge the players to further development, and the learning will be transferred to other games and life situations they encounter.

USE OF QUESTIONS

One way to help students learn game tactics and give verbal expression to what they are learning is to ask effective questions. Each game in this book includes a couple of important questions to get you started. As an example of the kinds of questions helpful in the TGfU approach, here is a list of questions for understanding regarding positional play:

• What are some things you or your team is having difficulty with?

• What are some strategies you can use to solve this?

• What can you see that other teams of players are doing well?

- What strategies can you use to help your team play better?
- In what ways can you create space?
- What are some different types of passes you can use?
- When is the best time to run with or dribble the ball?
- When is the best time to pass the ball?
- What are the roles and responsibilities of the different defensive and offensive players?
- How can you be more effective in your role?

By answering open-ended questions and dealing with tactical problems, participants will enhance many valuable skills, including individual reasoning. Because these problem-solving tasks are often done in small groups, the players' interpersonal skills and social reasoning skills should also improve. Teamwork requires helping others learn and holding each other accountable; these are also valuable skills. Through it all, the players learn to take responsibility for their learning, develop motor skills, enjoy physically active participation, and have a great deal of fun. The benefits of teaching games with the TGfU model are numerous and important.

TEACHING SUGGESTIONS

Children are shaped more by our actions than by our words, so we need to model our talk. Be sure to model the joy and importance of learning to be physically active and participating in the activities at hand. Take time for personal fitness development.

Go from the big game to a small part of it and then back to the big game again. For example, soccer is played by 11 players a side on a huge field. But much of the game is about the give-and-go between 2 players, keeping the ball away from a defender, and shooting accurately on the run. We made games out of these smaller parts of the bigger game. You may want to make your own games that are smaller yet or perhaps add a few more people and make the activity bigger and closer to the more formalized version of the game. Get your games going with enough rules and directions to purposively engage the children. Next, decide on the major areas for improvement. Build on those in smaller games, and then take them back to the bigger game. Remember that the individual skills and games are not as important as replicating these in bigger-game situations.

Take time to stop the play in order to discuss and solve problems of player alignment and distribution—for example, sometimes players are too close together, so there is no one to pass the ball to. Ask questions about skill and strategy so players understand the principles of games and the game at hand and take ownership of the solutions. Keep instructions short and simple so that students understand the main concepts and are guided and engaged in learning the activity.

At the end of each class, review the key components learned. Ask the players what they liked best in the lesson and how they would change any drills or activities to improve them. Ask them to invent a new game or drill to review the same skills. Finally, have the players do some stretches and then go for a short walk or easy jog to cool down.

EQUIPMENT SUGGESTIONS

Equipment need not be elaborate and can often be picked up inexpensively at garage sales, in thrift stores, or through online sites. Some regular sports equipment is helpful, including baseballs, baseball gloves, bats, a baseball tee, a badminton set, tennis equipment, plastic discs (Frisbees), soccer balls, bowling pins (or juice cans or water bottles), a football, and possibly some lacrosse sticks and rubber balls. As targets, garbage cans or other pails will do, and sometimes chalk can be used to draw targets on the pavement. Cones are great for obstacle courses, but beanbags or sponges also work. Some of the activities require timing, so have a watch, stopwatch, or cell phone on hand. In addition, objects such as pool noodles, balloons, and flags (ripped fabric strips in two colors) are helpful. Larger pieces of equipment such as trampolines, basketball hoops, and hockey goals are also helpful but not essential.

Measuring tapes could be used to measure and determine distances. In this book we have simplified things by just using steps. We think one step will roughly equal a small yard or a small meter.

OVERALL LEARNING EXPECTATIONS

It is important for both the learners and the teachers to know if the students are learning anything and if they are learning it correctly. Ideally, assessing student learning answers these questions and further encourages mastery over various skills.

Many jurisdictions have their own standards and expectations. In preparing this chapter, we selected two from the United States and Canada, the NASPE standards and the Ontario Ministry of Education's curriculum expectations. The basics of these two systems are listed in table 1.1.

Table 1.1 NASPE and Ontario Physical Education Standards

NASPE	Ontario
Standard 1: The physically literate individual demonstrates competency in a variety of motor skills and movement patterns.	**Perform movement skills,** demonstrating awareness of the basic requirements of the skills and applying movement concepts as appropriate, as they engage in a variety of physical activities.
Standard 2: The physically literate individual applies knowledge of concepts, principles, strategies, and tactics related to movement and performance.	**Apply movement strategies appropriately,** demonstrating an understanding of the components of a variety of physical activities, in order to enhance their ability to participate successfully in those activities.
Standard 3: The physically literate individual demonstrates the knowledge and skills to achieve and maintain a health-enhancing level of physical activity and fitness.	**Participate actively and regularly** in a wide variety of physical activities and identify how regular physical activity can be incorporated into their daily lives.
	Demonstrate an understanding of the importance of being physically active and apply physical fitness concepts and practices that contribute to healthy, active living.
Standard 4: The physically literate individual exhibits responsible personal and social behavior that respects self and others.	**Demonstrate responsibility** for their own safety and the safety of others as they participate in physical activities.
Standard 5: The physically literate individual recognizes the value of physical activity for health, enjoyment, challenge, self-expression, and/or social interaction.	**Demonstrate an understanding of factors** that contribute to their personal enjoyment of being active. Identify a variety of ways to be physically active at school and at home.

LESSON PLANNING

We have provided lesson plans based around skill themes for the entire year. Typically we grouped lessons so that similar skills are being taught for a two-week period. Each lesson begins with a warm-up game followed by a fitness activity, and then the lesson builds with three or four other related games—if you have three shorter classes, pick one activity per class. The end of the lesson is a good time to do some stretching exercises, discuss and review what was learned in the session, and slow the students' energy levels down so they are ready for the next class.

All the warm-up games and fitness games are described in chapter 2, and all the other games are found in chapters 3 through 6. Chapters

7 and 8 cover the topics of dance and gymnastics to provide a comprehensive program.

The program is designed for one year and is to be repeated for one more year. Children 5 and 6 years old do the same activity both years, children 7 and 8 years old do the same activity both years, and children 9 and 10 years old do the same activity both years. Each week, the type of skill or sport is the same for all the age groups to simplify teaching the same general content to everyone. It is our hope that the children can help each other with the different games. Expect considerable differences in ability if you are teaching children of different ages (e.g., 5 and 10 years old). However, the games are designed to be played with few players, and the challenges can be simplified for younger children and increased for older children to make a shared and equally challenging game possible for both. During weeks 4, 13, 16, 25, 28, and 35, we suggest trying some local fall, winter, spring, and summer activities suitable to your area, which may include such things as hiking, orienteering, cycling, swimming, tobogganing, and fitness testing. In our implementation of this resource, we have found that many of the activities can easily be modified for even older children than those in fifth grade.

Children + Outdoors = Physical Activity + Health

John Byl

What follows is a one-year menu for grades K and 1 (see table 1.2), 2 and 3 (see table 1.3), and 4 and 5 (see table 1.4).

Table 1.2 Lesson Plans for Children Aged 5 and 6 (Grades K and 1)

Week	Theme	Warm-up	Fitness	Activity 1	Activity 2	Activity 3
1	Introduction Fitness test					
2	Kick and receive: soccer	Up and Down	Fifty Percents (single)	Dribble Tag	Robin's Nest	Slow Dribbler
3	Kick and receive: soccer	Follow That Engine	Fifty Percents (double)	Hog	Tight-Quarter Dribble	Two-to-One Keep-Away
4	Fall outdoor: hike (with some ori-enteering), cycling trip					
5	Strike or hit and receive: softball	Soccer Baseball	Rock, Paper, Scissors Chase	Stepper-Board Catch — Three in a Row	Teeing Off	Throw for Points
6	Strike or hit and receive: softball	Noodle Paddle	Shuttle Run With Blocks	Long Accuracy Throws	Rollers	Teeing Off
7	Throw and receive: foot-ball	Hut	Cone Square	Catch What You Can	Fumble	Long Accuracy Throws
8	Throw and receive: foot-ball	Grid	Subtract a Jack	Grid Pass	Tail Tag	Nailing It
9	Movement: dance	Aerobic Routine	X Dance for warm-up	Dance Cards for Line Danc-ing	Eddie the Razor	X Dance for cool-down and stretching
10	Strike or hit and receive: volleyball	Passing Volleyballs	Kangaroos and Penguins	Beanbag Toss to Partner	Net Toss	Partner Net Toss: Balloon Net Whack
11	Strike or hit and receive: volleyball	Passing Vol-leyballs: Part-ner Passing	Bench Step-Ups	Net Toss	Forearm Four Square	Partner Net Toss: Balloon Net Whack
12	Movement: gymnastics	Running: see lesson plan	Plank Holds	Rolling Skills	Transference of Weight	Balancing Bodies
13	Optional: swimming, tobogganing, fitness test					

(continued)

Table 1.2 (continued)

Week	Theme	Warm-up	Fitness	Activity 1	Activity 2	Activity 3
14	Kick and receive: soccer (indoor, outdoor, in the snow?)	What Time Is It, Mr. Wolf?	Tabata Drills	Double Cone Ball	Long Trap	Speed Trap
15	Kick and receive: soccer (indoor, outdoor, in the snow?)	Partner Pass	Bench Push-ups and Triceps Dips	Double Cone Ball	Two Goal-keepers	Timed Ball Kicks
16	Winter outdoor					
17	Throw and receive: bowling	Up and Down	Medicine Ball Pass	Long Accuracy Rolls	Miss the Pins	Five-Pin Blaster
18	Throw and receive: basketball	Follow That Engine	Jump Rope	Partner Pass	Sprinters	Stepper-Board Catch
19	Movement: dance	Aerobic Routine	X Dance for warm-up	Dance Cards for Line Dancing	Eddie the Razor	X Dance for cool-down and stretching
20	Strike or hit and receive: hockey	What Time Is It, Mr. Wolf?	Up and Down	Quick Relay Pass	He Shoots, He Scores	Double Cone Ball
21	Strike or hit and receive: hockey	What Time Is It, Mr. Wolf?	Body Parts	Obstacle Dribble	Timed Wall Dribble	Offensive Attack
22	Movement: gymnastics	Running: see lesson plan	Medicine Ball Pass	Rolling Skills	Transference of Weight	Balancing Bodies
23	Throw and receive: basketball	Up and Down	Alligators	Freestyle Discs	Hog	Tight-Quarter Dribble
24	Throw and receive: basketball	What Time Is It, Mr. Wolf?	Kangaroos and Penguins	Freestyle Discs	Hog	Tight-Quarter Dribble
25	Optional: swimming, tobogganing, fitness test					
26	Kick and receive: soccer	Follow That Engine	Subtract a Jack	Timed Wall Dribble	Speed Trap	Rolling Goals
27	Disc	Tail Ball	Bench Step-Ups	Freestyle Discs	Disc Archery	Record for Distance

Week	Theme	Warm-up	Fitness	Activity 1	Activity 2	Activity 3
28	Spring outdoor					
29	Movement: track and field	Fartleks	Alligators	Engage in various running, jumping, and throwing events		
30	Movement: track and field	Fartleks	Rock, Paper, Scissors Chase	Engage in various running, jumping, and throwing events.		
31	Throw and receive: lacrosse	Partner Pass	Tabata Drills	Catch What You Can	Quick Relay Pass	Long Accuracy Throws
32	Throw and receive: lacrosse	Partner Pass	Up and Down	Wall Spike	Freestyle Discs	He Shoots, He Scores
33 Option 1	Strike or hit and receive: badminton	Up and Down	Cone Square	Record for Maximum Time Aloft	Nailing It	Disc Golf
33 Option 2	Strike or hit and receive: tennis	Up and Down	Cone Square	Balance Race	Slalom Course	No-Net Consecutive Hits
34 Option 1	Strike or hit and receive: badminton	Up and Down	Fifty Percents (single, double)	Record for Maximum Time Aloft	Nailing It	Disc Golf
34 Option 2	Strike or hit and receive: tennis	Up and Down	Fifty Percents (single, double)	No-Net Consecutive Hits	Drop Ball	Wall Ball
35	Optional: swimming, cycling, fitness test					

Table 1.3 Lesson Plans for Children Aged 7 and 8 (Grades 2 and 3)

Week	Theme	Warm-up	Fitness	Activity 1	Activity 2	Activity 3
1	Introduction Fitness test					
2	Kick and receive: soccer	Partner Pass	Fifty Percents (single)	Card Bouncers	Robin's Nest	Dribble Tag
3	Kick and receive: soccer	Disc Golf: Speed Golf	Fifty Percents (double)	Hog	Two-to-One Keep-Away	Sliders
4	Fall outdoor: hike (with some ori-enteering), cycling trip					
5	Strike or hit and receive: softball	Soccer Base-ball	Rock, Paper, Scissors Chase	Throw for Points	Hot Box	Five Hundred
6	Strike or hit and receive: softball	In-the-Ball-park Home Runs	Shuttle Run With Blocks	Long Accuracy Throws	Quick Relay Pass	No-Defense Running
7	Throw and receive: foot-ball	Hut	Cone Square	Catch What You Can	Mirror	Fumble
8	Throw and receive: foot-ball	Grid	Subtract a Jack	Grid Pass	Tail Tag	Two-to-One Keep-Away
9	Movement: dance	Aerobic Routine	X Dance for warm-up	Dance Cards for Line Danc-ing	Cumbia Urbana	X Dance for cool-down and stretching
10	Strike or hit and receive: volleyball	Passing Volleyballs	Kangaroos and Penguins	Passing Volleyballs: Partner Continuous Passing	Partner Net Toss	Passing Vol-leyballs: Trian-gle Passing
11	Strike or hit and receive: volleyball	Passing Volleyballs: Partner Passing	Bench Step-Ups	Beanbag Toss to Partner: Serve a Ball to Partner	Wall Spike	Wall Spike: Continuous Wall Spike (also do with partners)
12	Movement: gymnastics	Running: see lesson plan	Plank Holds	Rolling Skills	Transference of Weight	Balancing Bodies
13	Optional: swimming, tobogganing, fitness test					

Week	Theme	Warm-up	Fitness	Activity 1	Activity 2	Activity 3
14	Kick and receive: soccer (indoor, outdoor, in the snow?)	Running Circles	Tabata Drills	Two-Player Bowling	Speed Trap	Soccer Baseball
15	Kick and receive: soccer (indoor, outdoor, in the snow?)	Partner Pass	Bench Push-Ups and Triceps Dips	Double Cone Ball	Two-on-One Keep-Away	Soccer Baseball: Soccer Baseball With Dribble
16	Winter outdoor					
17	Throw and receive: bowling	Up and Down	Medicine Ball Pass	Two-Player Bowling	Miss the Pins	Five-Pin Blaster
18	Throw and receive: basketball	Dribble Tag	Jump Rope	Partner Pass	Sprinters	Timed Ball Kicks
19	Movement: dance	Aerobic Routine	X Dance for warm-up	Dance Cards for Line Dancing	Cumbia Urbana	X Dance for cool-down and stretching
20	Strike or hit and receive: hockey	Follow That Engine	Up and Down	Card Bouncers	He Shoots, He Scores	Double Cone Ball
21	Strike or hit and receive: hockey	Partner Pass	Body Parts	Obstacle Dribble	Quick Relay Pass	Offensive Attack
22	Movement: gymnastics	Running: see lesson plan	Medicine Ball Pass	Rolling Skills	Transference of Weight	Balancing Bodies
23	Throw and receive: basketball	Fit Circle	Alligators	Freestyle Discs	Hog	Tight-Quarter Dribble
24	Throw and receive: basketball	Running Circles	Kangaroos and Penguins	Obstacle Dribble	Offensive Attack	Tight-Quarter Dribble: Tight-Quarter Dribble With an It
25	Optional: swimming, tobogganing, fitness test					
26	Kick and receive: soccer	Split Triangle Run	Subtract a Jack	Timed Wall Dribble	Speed Trap	Rolling Goals

(continued)

Table 1.3 (*continued*)

Week	Theme	Warm-up	Fitness	Activity 1	Activity 2	Activity 3
27	Disc	Tail Ball	Bench Step-Ups	Nailing It	Record for Distance	Disc Golf
28	Spring outdoor					
29	Movement: track and field	Fartleks	Alligators	Engage in various running, jumping, and throwing events.		
30	Movement: track and field	Fartleks	Rock, Paper, Scissors Chase	Engage in various running, jumping, and throwing events.		
31	Throw and receive: lacrosse	Partner Pass	Tabata Drills	Wall Spike: Continuous Wall Spike	Quick Relay Pass	Long Accuracy Throws
32	Throw and receive: lacrosse	Split Triangle Run	Up and Down	Wall Spike: Continuous Wall Spike (with partner)	Card Bouncers	He Shoots, He Scores
33 Option 1	Strike or hit and receive: badminton	Follow That Engine	Cone Square	Disc Archery	Record For Maximum Time Aloft	Disc Golf
33 Option 2	Strike or hit and receive: tennis	Follow That Engine	Cone Square	No-Net Consecutive Hits: Consecutive Hits With a Net *or* Long Hits	Wall Ball	Distance Wall Ball, or Partners Wall Ball
34	Strike or hit and receive: badminton	Follow That Engine	Fifty Percents (single, double)	Disc Archery	Record For Maximum Time Aloft	Disc Golf: Speed Golf
35	Optional: swimming, cycling, fitness test					

Table 1.4 Lesson Plans for Children Aged 9 and 10 (Grades 4 and 5)

Week	Theme	Warm-up	Fitness	Activity 1	Activity 2	Activity 3
1	Introduction Fitness test					
2	Kick and receive: soccer	Grid Pass	Fifty Percents (single)	Sprinters	Robin's Nest	Dribble Tag
3	Kick and receive: soccer	Passing Threes	Fifty Percents (double)	Hog	Two-to-One Keep-Away	Sliders
4	Fall outdoor: hike (with some orienteering), cycling trip					
5	Strike or hit and receive: softball	Soccer Baseball	Rock, Paper, Scissors Chase	Throw for Points and Hot Box	Five Hundred	Disc Golf
6	Strike or hit and receive: softball	In-the-Ballpark Home Runs	Shuttle Run With Blocks	Throw for Points and Quick Relay Pass	Baseball Without Baserunning	Ghost Baseball
7	Throw and receive: football	Hut	Cone Square	Catch What You Can	Mirror	Hit It Down or Intercept
8	Throw and receive: football	Grid	Subtract a Jack	Grid Pass	Tail Tag	Long Accuracy Throws
9	Movement: dance	Aerobic Routine	X Dance for warm-up	Dance Cards for Line Dancing	Don't Sit Still (from YouTube)	Ethno Tension (from YouTube)
10	Strike or hit and receive: volleyball	Passing Volleyballs	Kangaroos and Penguins	Passing Volleyballs: Partner Continuous Passing	Mini Volleyball	Passing Volleyballs: Triangle Passing
11	Strike or hit and receive: volleyball	Passing Threes	Bench Step-Ups	Beanbag Toss to Partner: Serve a Ball to Partner	Wall Spike	Wall Spike: Continuous Wall Spike
12	Movement: gymnastics	Running: see lesson plan	Plank Holds	Rolling Skills	Transference of Weight	Balancing Bodies

(continued)

Table 1.4 *(continued)*

Week	Theme	Warm-up	Fitness	Activity 1	Activity 2	Activity 3
13	Optional: swimming, tobogganing. fitness test					
14	Kick and receive: soccer (indoor, outdoor, in the snow?)	Running Circles	Tabata Drills	Dribble Tag	Tight-Quarter Dribble: Tight-Quarter Dribble With an It	Soccer Billiards
15	Kick and receive: soccer (indoor, outdoor, in the snow?)	Split Triangle Run	Bench Push-Ups and Triceps Dips	Split Triangle Run: Thrown-In	Two-on-One Keep-Away	Soccer Baseball: Soccer Baseball With Dribble
16	Winter outdoor					
17	Throw and receive: bowling	Up and Down	Medicine Ball Pass	Two-Player Bowling	Miss the Pins	Ten-Pin Slam
18	Throw and receive: basketball	Passing Threes	Jump Rope	Partner Pass	Sprinters	Timed Wall Dribble
19	Movement: dance	Aerobic Routine	X Dance for warm-up	Dance Cards for Line Dancing	Don't Sit Still (from YouTube)	Ethno Tension (from YouTube)
20	Strike or hit and receive: hockey	Follow That Engine	Up and Down	Card Bouncers	He Shoots, He Scores	Double Cone Ball
21	Strike or hit and receive: hockey	Partner Pass	Body Parts	Obstacle Dribble	Passing Threes	Offensive Attack
22	Movement: gymnastics	Running: see lesson plan	Medicine Ball Pass	Rolling Skills	Transference of Weight	Balancing Bodies
23	Throw and receive: basketball	Quick Relay Pass	Alligators	Mirror	Obstacle Dribble	Tight-Quarter Dribble

Week	Theme	Warm-up	Fitness	Activity 1	Activity 2	Activity 3
24	Throw and receive: basketball	Split Triangle Run	Kangaroos and Penguins	Throw for Points	Offensive Attack	Tight-Quarter Dribble: Tight-Quarter Dribble With an It
25	Optional: swimming, tobogganing, fitness test					
26	Kick and receive: soccer	Split Triangle Run	Subtract a Jack	Timed Wall Dribble	Speed Trap	Rolling Goals
27	Disc	Record for Throw, Run, and Catch	Bench Step-Ups	Record for Maximum Time Aloft	Walling for Distance	Double Disc Court
28	Spring outdoor					
29	Movement: track and field	Fartleks	Alligators	Engage in various running, jumping, and throwing events.		
30	Movement: track and field	Fartleks	Rock, Paper, Scissors Chase	Engage in various running, jumping, and throwing events.		
31	Throw and receive: lacrosse	Partner Pass	Tabata Drills	Wall Spike: Continuous Wall Spike	Timed Throw and Score	Long Accuracy Throws
32	Throw and receive: lacrosse	Split Triangle Run	Up and Down	Partner Wall Spike	Card Bouncers	He Shoots, He Scores
33	Strike or hit and receive: badminton	Split Triangle Run	Cone Square	Record for Throw, Run, and Catch	Double Disc Court	Speedminton www.speedminton.ca/
34	Strike or hit and receive: badminton	Fit Circle	Fifty Percents (single, double)	Record for Throw, Run, and Catch	Double Disc Court	Speedminton www.speedminton.ca/
35	Optional: swimming, cycling, fitness test					

2

WARM-UP, COOL-DOWN, AND FITNESS GAMES

Nothing happens until something moves.

Albert Einstein

It is helpful to warm up before an activity, cool down after an activity, limber up before an activity, and stretch after an activity. This chapter briefly highlights the benefits of warm-ups and cool-downs, briefly explains the theory of stretching, and provides a set of warm-up and cool-down games that are fun and related to the activities at hand. Physical fitness is also important, and although most of the lessons can be quite active, the games used for warm-ups and for the fitness section specifically focus on physical fitness. This chapter briefly touches on cardiorespiratory and muscular endurance, muscular strength, flexibility, and body composition. The bulk of the chapter consists of cardio activities that can be used for warm-ups, for fitness, and for cool-downs (just done at half speed for cool-downs). There is also a smaller section of games devoted to warm-up, cool-down, and fitness activities that involve strength training.

WARM-UP

For purposes of the lessons in this book, about 5 minutes is ample time for warm-up and limbering activities. The lessons are structured to begin with a 5-minute warm-up activity immediately followed by a fitness activity—the games are interchangeable, as a warm-up is meant to get the body moving and warmed up. These two activities usually take less than 10 minutes and adequately prepare the students for the lesson that follows. From a time and teaching perspective, try to relate the warm-up to the activity for that day.

The benefits of an effective warm-up include the following (Byl 2004, 4):

- Reduces the risk of injury
- Gradually increases heart rate and blood circulation
- Increases body temperature
- Improves efficiency of muscular actions
- Improves transmission of nerve impulses
- Permits freer movements in the joints
- Prepares the joints and associated muscles to function through their full range of motion
- Aids psychological preparation for the activity to follow

COOL-DOWN

At the end of an active class, practice, or contest, a cool-down is helpful to return the body temperature to normal and assist in recovering from the activity. The cool-down usually lasts for 3 to 5 minutes. If the place you are participating in the activity is a few minutes' walk from your home, then the walk home will serve well for a cool-down. Otherwise doing one of the warm-up games, but at half speed, or going for a 3- to 5-minute walk will serve the participants well.

An effective cool-down does the following (Byl 2004, 7):

- Decreases the heart rate and blood circulation gradually
- Aids venous return (by maintaining contraction of the leg muscles to help prevent blood from pooling in the legs and to assist the return of blood to the heart)
- Assists in the removal of waste products (particularly lactic acid, which may have built up as a by-product of vigorous anaerobic work such as sprinting or jumping), allowing a quicker and more comfortable recovery from exercise
- Helps minimize postexercise muscle stiffness and soreness
- Returns the body safely and effectively to a preexercise condition

STRETCHING

The main purposes of stretching are to reduce injury, enhance performance through increased flexibility of the muscles and tendons, and develop lifelong flexibility. Although stretching is often done as part of the warm-up, research does not support this practice. The research suggests that stretching during a warm-up will decrease performance, and therefore stretching should be done after the activity and as part of a program to develop lifelong flexibility. The general recommendations are that players stretch three times per week, preferably after some activity, and the stretches be moved into slowly and held for 15 to 30 seconds.

Following are several key teaching points that are useful in teaching stretching (Byl 2004, 9-10):

- Ease into the stretch slowly.
- Hold the stretch still—do not bounce.
- Feel mild tension in the middle of the stretched muscle.
- If you feel any pain or the muscle starts shaking, ease off the stretch immediately.
- Relax all other parts of your body, particularly your head, shoulders, and back.
- Don't fight against the muscle; try to relax.
- If comfortable, and the muscle feels relaxed, try increasing the stretch gently and holding the new position still.
- Gently ease out of the stretch.

The exception to not stretching is when you are participating in activities that will push a joint beyond its normal range of motion. Such activities include gymnastics, wrestling, and diving. Limbering up through dynamic stretching can be an important part of any warm-up. Dynamic stretching involves moving parts of your body and gradually increasing reach, speed of movement, or both. Most of the time the body is stretched through the movement, and typically the stretch is not held for more than 2 seconds. These movements are repeated 8 to 15 times. Examples include such activities as arm circles, leg swings, leg lunges, and moving along the ground as an inch worm. There are many examples of this on the Internet. Two excellent sources are http://en.wikipedia.org/wiki/Dynamic_stretching and youtube.com/watch?v=DkCZym9CT54.

WHAT IS FITNESS?

It is helpful from the perspective of both developing a positive lifestyle and improving current fitness to engage children in fitness activities as part of their daily routines. The major way we try to encourage fitness development is through the games and activities suggested during each lesson. However, some specific fitness activities are also helpful, and those are addressed in this chapter. We briefly discuss the physiology of various fitness components—cardiorespiratory fitness, muscular strength, muscular endurance, and flexibility—and then make some suggestions for developing these types of fitness.

Cardiorespiratory Fitness

During the growing years, cardiorespiratory endurance progressively improves because of increased running efficiency, increased muscular endurance, and physiological changes. In terms of physiological adaptations, the most notable is an increase in size of the heart muscle, which results in an increased volume of blood pumped throughout the body with each heartbeat. Resting heart rate is one measure of cardiorespiratory fitness, and it will decrease with age during the childhood years, simply because the child's body is growing. However, helping children enjoy being active will also improve their endurance.

In terms of cardiorespiratory training, the overall expectation for optimal health is that children remain active for 90 minutes a day in 10-minute blocks. One of the simple ways to increase this time is to gradually decrease screen time (computer, television) and increase activity time (e.g., by encouraging children to go outside to play). A side benefit of running is increased bone density. Research suggests that children engaged in running and strength training activities show an increase in bone mineral density. These children tend to have fewer injuries, which may be attributable to increased bone density as well as increased motor coordination.

Muscular Strength

Muscular strength is the ability of a muscle, or group of muscles, to apply force at near-maximal levels of exertion. Strength is necessary for children so they can carry objects and support their own body weight on playground equipment. In games, muscular strength is helpful for such things as shooting or blocking an opponent from going past.

The number of muscle fibers a person has is fixed at birth; any increase in muscle size is due to an increase in the size of existing muscle fibers. As children grow, particularly boys, the proportion of muscle to body mass increases, which makes them stronger. The hormonal systems of prepubescent children are immature, and therefore strength gains during this period typically have more to do with increased efficiency of muscle contraction and increased motor skill coordination than they do with actual strengthening of the muscle.

Muscular Endurance

Muscular endurance is the ability of a muscle, or group of muscles, to repeatedly apply submaximal force for a relatively long time. Most activities that are completed over a longer period require muscular endurance. The factors affecting muscular endurance are similar to those explained in the paragraph on muscular strength.

Muscular strength and endurance training should focus on helping children understand their bodies, promoting lifetime fitness, maintaining a positive attitude toward training, and engaging children in fun activities. When engaged in specific training, it is more important to have children perform many repetitions than it is to increase the load and decrease the number of repetitions. Most training can be done by playing a variety of games or using the children's own body weight (e.g., through such activities as push-ups, sit-ups, squats, and wall sits).

Flexibility

Flexibility is joint specific and involves the range of motion for a specific joint. It is important for activities as simple as bending down to pick up objects and for more sport-specific purposes as giving greater strength to a movement because of the larger range of motion in specific joints. Range of motion is typically at its peak for children aged 6 through 10 and decreases into adulthood. In the prepubertal period, marked by extensive growth, flexibility tends to greatly decrease because the bones are growing more rapidly than the tendons (it is the tendons that largely determine the extent of a person's flexibility). Because of the effect of the hormones estrogen and progesterone on connective tissue extensibility, females tend to be more flexible than males. Stretching is the best way to develop flexibility.

Body Composition

Body composition is another important attribute of total fitness. Our bodies are categorized into two main groups of tissues: lean mass (muscles, bones, ligaments, and organs) and fat mass (essential and stored fat). We all require a minimum level of essential fat to protect and insulate nervous system tissues and the heart, lungs, intestines, kidneys, and muscles. Fat also stores several nutrients. Essential fat plays an additional and important role in females in terms of hormonal production, menstruation, bone development, and child bearing. Males should have 3 to 5 percent of body mass as essential fat, and females should have 10 to 15 percent. Most storage fat is located under the surface of the skin. Although a certain amount of storage fat is helpful for body insulation, for protective padding, and as an energy reserve, too much storage fat is unhealthy and contributes to cardiovascular diseases, hypertension, and diabetes.

Assessing body composition correctly requires some training and precise tools. Fat cells laid down in one's youth tend to remain for a lifetime. Wise parents will know when their child is obese and take appropriate steps to help the child deal with this issue. Wise parents will also know when a child is perfectly healthy and that comments about the child's weight (especially for girls) can lead to a variety of deadly eating disorders. The prime considerations for parents around issues of body composition have to do with eating healthy foods and being active. Healthy lifestyles will lead to proper body composition; drastic dietary changes (assuming the foods the child is eating are healthy) will likely increase health problems.

Fitness Tests

Graphing children's fitness scores a few times per year is helpful. Typically children will improve because of physical maturation, but attributing some of the improvement to their effort will reinforce the importance of daily physical activity. Doing a fitness test every three months can be a positive motivator to keep active—particularly when the scores are measured against past performance.

Fitness tests typically include measurements of cardiorespiratory fitness, flexibility, abdominal strength and endurance, upper-body strength and endurance, and body composition. The beep test is a common measurement tool for cardiorespiratory fitness. The test consists of completing 20-meter runs more quickly until the student cannot do it anymore. Many cell phones will have a free app that can be downloaded to provide the correct beep times along with some interpretation of the results. Flexibility is joint specific, but most fitness tests measure flexibility of the lower back and hamstring muscles through the sit-and-reach test.

Abdominal strength and endurance is typically tested by having the child perform sit-ups while lying on the floor, with knees flexed and a partner sitting on the feet to anchor them to the ground; the one being tested slides her hands along the floor to a marker underneath her knees or slides her hands down her leg to touch her knee. Upper-body strength and endurance is often tested with some variation of a flexed arm hang—holding a bar with arms bent and chin at the level of the bar, the child holds this position as long as possible. Probably the simplest way, but not always totally accurate, to assess body composition is to look at height and weight charts (these can easily be found online) or to use a body mass index (BMI) calculator designed for children such as the one found at http://apps.nccd.cdc.gov/dnpabmi.

BENCH STEP-UPS

Objective

To complete the greatest number of step-ups in 1 minute

Specific Skill Focus

Step-ups

Equipment

A low bench, or a park bench, or a curb and a timing device (for safety reasons, ensure the bench is securely bolted to the ground)

Setup

The players stand facing a bench.

How to Play

- At a signal from the leader, the players step up onto the bench with one foot and then step the second foot up so they are standing on the bench.
- The players then step down one foot at a time, continuing this stepping up and down motion, counting steps up, until the leader signals that 1 minute has passed.

Variations

- If the bench or curb is low enough, players jump up and down with both feet, or up with both and down with one foot at a time.
- Players can change body positions so they are sideways to the bench and do half the step-ups from one side and half from the other side.

Questions for Understanding

- Is it easier to look at the bench or to look straight ahead when stepping up and down?
- How do different arm motions assist your step-ups?

BODY PARTS

Objective

To be the fastest and most accurate pair of runners

Specific Skill Focus

Running, slowing down, control

Equipment

Cones

Setup

- Set up two rows of cones, about 30 feet (10 steps) apart.
- Players divide themselves into pairs, with one player at one line and the other player at the other line.

How to Play

- At the leader's signal and call of a body part, the pairs of runners run toward each other, meeting in the middle or wherever they meet (this way slower and often younger runners do not need to run as far) and touching the body part called out. For example, if the leader calls, "Elbows," the runners slow their run to touch elbows and then run back to their respective cone lines as fast as they can.
- The winning pair is the pair with both players at their lines first. The leader can simply keep calling body parts to keep the players running.

Variations

- Add a memory challenge by asking the players to add on to each previous part. If the first time they touched elbows, then the second time they would touch elbows first and then the second body part, such as knees. Keep adding on until the players can't keep it all straight.
- Change the method of movement, adding hopping, two-foot jumping, sideways shuffle.

- Increase or decrease the distance between the running pairs.
- The players can do manipulative skills while running such as dribbling a ball, bouncing a tennis ball on a racket, or bouncing a ping-pong ball on a plastic disc.

Questions for Understanding

- Where can you be looking to help your stop be more accurate?
- How can you change the weighting on your feet for a faster start to your run?

CONE SQUARE

Objective

To follow the leader around the cones

Specific Skill Focus

Movement changes, speed changes, direction changes (e.g., forward, sideways)

Equipment

Four cones

Setup

- Set up the cones to form a large square.
- The distance between cones can be from about 3 steps to about 10 steps.
- Identify which two opposite sides are the ends and which are the sides.
- The players line up behind the leader.

How to Play

- Moving around the outside of the square, the leader calls out a movement, such as "Jog on the ends" and "Side-shuffle on the sides," and the group does this a few times.
- Then the leader changes one command, such as "Change the ends to walking lunges" or "Jog the ends and sprint the sides," and the group follows.

Variations

- Change the leader to allow other players to lead.
- Add other cones, such as a single cone off one corner, and instruct the group to run and touch that cone each time they hit that corner cone.
- Change the shape into a rectangle.
- Dribble a ball while moving.

Questions for Understanding

- How can you vary a move like the side shuffle to challenge each leg equally?
- How can you vary the intensity to stay challenged but still be in control of your breathing?

EVERYONE IT: SNATCH PINS

Objective

To gain as many clothespins as possible

Specific Skill Focus

General warm-up

Equipment

Five clothespins per player

Setup

Each player (you will need at least three) puts five clothespins on the lower back of their shirts.

How to Play

- On the signal to begin, the players try to remove a clothespin from one of the other competitors while moving to avoid having their clothespins stolen—players cannot protect their clothespins in any way other than by moving their bodies.

- Once a player has taken one or more clothespins off a competitor, that player kneels and puts the clothespins on the back of his shirt—while a player is doing this, no other player can steal a clothespin from him. Once the clothespin is attached, the player must immediately stand and resume play.

- If a player has no clothespins, that player can continue to try to remove clothespins.

- After a set time, stop the game and count the number of clothespins each player has. The one with the most is the winner.

Variation

If there are many people playing this game, try having them work in teams of two or more, and then count how many clothespins the teams can collect.

Questions for Understanding

- What are effective ways to protect clothespins while trying to remove clothespins from others?
- How can this game be made easier or harder? Slower or faster?

Note: Additional clothespin games can be found at www.youthwork-practice.com/games/clothespins-games.html.

FARTLEKS

Objective

To jog while dribbling a ball, maintaining distance between players and quickly increasing speed when it is your turn to run from the back

Specific Skill Focus

General warm-up or specifically for basketball, soccer, hockey, or badminton (instead of dribbling a ball, bounce a shuttle on a racket while doing this game)

Equipment

One ball per player

Setup

The players line up behind a leader, leaving one or two steps of distance between each player.

How to Play

- The leader starts the group at a slow jogging pace.
- All players dribble and keep the balls (or shuttles) close to themselves.
- The last player in line sprints to the front of the line and becomes the leader, and then she slows back down to a slow jogging pace.
- As soon as that player is in the lead position, the new last player takes off for the front.
- This pattern continues until everyone has had a turn or until the group has completed a specified distance (e.g., once around a soccer field).

Variation

Use one ball for the whole group. The leader begins with the ball. He maintains the running pace and passes the ball back to the next player in line. That player has a set number of contacts with the ball (two or more) and then passes it back to the next player, until finally the last player gets the ball and then powers up to the front.

Questions for Understanding

- How can the team help the back player best move to the front of the line?
- What role does effective communication with teammates serve during the activity?

FIFTY PERCENTS (SINGLE)

Objective

To change direction and follow a pattern of moves through cones

Specific Skill Focus

Direction changes, squats, jumps

Equipment

Four cones per player

Setup

Line up four cones per player, spacing them one step apart. The player starts facing the first cone.

How to Play

- For the first set:
  - The player performs a side shuffle from the first to the second cone, touches the second cone, then shuffles back to touch the first cone.
  - The player then shuffles to and touches the third cone and returns to the first.
  - Finally, the player side-shuffles out to the fourth cone, touches it, and then side-shuffles back and touches the first cone.
- For the second set, the player repeats the same pattern but changes the movement to forward and backward running, still touching each cone.
- For the third set, the player returns to a sideways shuffle but adds a plyometric jump (double hop) after each cone touch.

Variations

- Change the distance between the cones.
- Change the pattern of the cones from a straight line to a zigzag.
- Add more cones to make the drill longer.
- Place a tennis ball on top of each cone; players collect the balls rather than touch the cones.

Questions for Understanding

- How does lowering your center of gravity change your shuffling or running?
- How do you know when your center of gravity is too low?

FIFTY PERCENTS (DOUBLE)

Objective

To change direction and follow a pattern of moves through cones

Specific Skill Focus

Direction changes, squats, jumps

Equipment

Four cones per pair of players

Setup

Line up four cones per pair, spacing them one or two steps apart. The players face each other over the first cone.

How to Play

- For the first set:
  - The players perform a side shuffle from the first to the second cone, touch the second cone, then shuffle back to touch the first cone.
  - The players then shuffle to and touch the third cone and return to the first.
  - Finally, the players side-shuffle out to the fourth cone, touch it, and then side-shuffle back and touch the first cone.
- For the second set, the players repeat the same pattern but change the movement to forward and backward running, still touching each cone.
- For the third set, the players return to sideways shuffle but add a plyometric jump and a "high ten," slapping both hands at the top of the jump after each cone touch.
- Throughout this drill, the players must move at the same pace as their partners.

Variations

- Change the distance between the cones.
- Change the pattern of the cones from a straight line to a zigzag.

- Add more cones to make the drill longer.
- Add a second pair of players to the group and challenge them to all remain together.

Questions for Understanding

- Is it helpful to talk to your partner as you hit each cone?
- When you jump for the high-ten hand slaps, how can you ensure you are both in the same place at the same time?

FIT CIRCLE

Objective

To successfully make passes

Specific Skill Focus

General warm-up or specifically for basketball, soccer, hockey, or badminton (instead of passing a ball, bounce a shuttle on a racket while doing this game)

Equipment

One soccer ball per group

Setup

- Players stand in a circle; five or seven players is ideal.
- One player has the ball.

How to Play

- The player with the ball passes the ball to the second player to her right.
- That player traps the ball and passes the ball to the second player to his right.
- The players continue passing until the ball returns to the original player.

Variation

Fit Circle with running: Once a player has passed the ball, she runs around the outside of the circle and returns in time to receive the next pass; she then passes the ball to the next player, who should be in place.

Questions for Understanding

- How can players most effectively pass and trap the balls and get around the circle in time?
- If a receiver is delayed, how can you make a pass that gives the receiver more time to receive the pass?

FLIPPING YOUR LIDS

Objective

To have more cones down than up or up than down depending on your task

Specific Skill Focus

General warm-up or used specifically for basketball, soccer, hockey, or badminton (instead of dribbling a ball, bounce a shuttle on a racket while doing this game)

Equipment

One ball, racket and shuttle, or hockey stick and ball per player and 20 cones

Setup

- Spread out the cones, with half in an upright position and half lying on their sides.
- Assign one player (or team) to set all the cones upright and the other player (or team) to knock them all over (if you have more than two players, assign an even number per team or two younger children against one older one).

How to Play

- On the signal to begin, players dribble the ball around the playing area and either set the cones upright or knock them over depending on their assignment.
- After a preset time limit, see which player (or team) has the most cones set up or knocked over.

Variation

Instead of using cones, use two-sided sponge scrubbers, which you can purchase 15 for a dollar at many dollar stores, or even scrap paper that has writing on one side and is blank on the other (be sure to recycle after use), or plastic lids from yogurt containers. Players turn these items over so their assigned side is up.

Questions for Understanding

- How can you most effectively dribble the quickest to the targets in the playing area?
- Is it more effective to flip cones that are close together or to do the stray ones first?

FOLLOW THAT ENGINE

Objective

To travel while dribbling the ball, maintaining a constant distance between yourself and the player in front of you

Specific Skill Focus

General warm-up or specifically for basketball, soccer, hockey, or badminton (instead of dribbling a ball, bounce a shuttle on a racket while doing this game)

Equipment

One ball, racket and shuttle, or hockey stick and ball per player

Setup

- Assign one player to be the "engine" at the front of the "train" of players.
- Everyone else lines up behind the engine, leaving about one or two steps between each player.

How to Play

The lead player takes off, keeping his ball under tight control, and the other players try to maintain their distance from the players in front of them while dribbling.

Variations

- Call out, "Faster!" or "Slower!" to have the engine vary its speed. Or instruct the engine to change speeds regularly to challenge the other players to watch for the speed changes.
- Yell out, "Caboose!" and everyone has to turn their balls around and begin following the last player.

Questions for Understanding

- How can you best control the ball and also keep track of the leader?
- How can the engine make things more difficult for the followers?

FUMBLE

Objective

To get an idea of what it feels like to recover a fumble

Specific Skill Focus

Picking up objects while running (football)

Equipment

One football for two or three players

Set up

Two or three players stand on a line, with one player holding the football.

How to Play

- Players jog the width of a field.
- One player makes a small throw of the ball ahead of the next runner as if it is a fumble.
- The player closest to the ball recovers the fumble.
- The goal is to gain control of the ball as quickly as possible.
- Once this player picks up the ball, she makes a small throw of the ball ahead of the next runner and then continues in this manner across the field and back.

Variation

The player recovering the ball falls on it instead of trying to pick it up.

Questions for Understanding

- Which way did you find was easier to control (pick up) the ball?
- Which way did you find better guarantees maintaining possession (i.e., not immediately dropping the ball again)?

GRID

Objectives

To not get caught in the middle

Specific Skill Focus

All sports

Equipment

Four markers per group

Setup

Make a square four steps across; four players are positioned at the four corners, and one player is in the middle of the square—if you have four players, form a triangle shape; form a pentagon with six players.

How to Play

- On the middle player's signal ("Go"), all players switch corners.
- When players switch, the middle player tries to get an open corner.
- If two players are tied, they play a quick game of rock, paper, scissors, with the winner getting the corner.
- The player without a corner goes to the middle and says, "Go." Continue.

Variations

- No-Call Grid: The middle player does not call the move. Instead, players in the corners try to switch places when the middle player is farther away or not looking. Once a player leaves a spot, she cannot immediately go back to it.
- Grids With Eight: Two adjacent squares join into one game. There are eight markers for eight players. Two players are in the middle who try to move onto any vacant marker.
- All Spots: Players try to be the first to get to all the spots.

Questions for Understanding

- What is the best way to get a spot when you are in the middle?
- What is the best way to keep a spot when moving away from your corner?

IN-THE-BALLPARK HOME RUNS

Objective

To count how many runs can be scored in 2 minutes

Specific Skill Focus

Baseball, softball, soccer, basketball, hockey, and lacrosse

Equipment

Four cones, a ball, and a timing device

Setup

- Place the four cones like bases for a baseball game.
- The two runners are at home plate, one holding the ball.

How to Play

- At the signal to begin, the runner with the ball runs around the four bases, tagging each one.
- When the runner returns home, he gives the ball to the player who is waiting.
- The second runner runs the bases and gives the ball to the first player, who has had a brief rest while the other runner was running the bases.
- Each lap counts for one run.
- Count how many runs can be scored in 2 minutes.

Variation

Dribble around the bases with a soccer ball or basketball or hockey puck or lacrosse ball.

Questions for Understanding

- How can you get the most efficient angles when running around the bases?
- How can a pair of players have the most efficient and effective exchange of equipment?

JUMP ROPE

Objective

To jump rope for a set time

Specific Skill Focus

Turning and jumping

Equipment

One jump rope per player, music player (optional)

Setup

Players spread themselves out from one another, leaving enough room to turn their ropes.

How to Play

- At a signal from the leader, the players begin to jump rope at a moderate pace.
- The leader calls out changes such as "slower" or "faster" or "one foot" or "two feet," and the players follow the instructions.

Skip with variations.

Variations

- Have the whole group move forward while jumping rope.
- For a player with coordination challenges, have him hold both rope ends in one hand and swing the rope on one side of his body.
- Have two players skip in pairs, side by side, with player one holding her right rope handle in her right hand and player two's right rope handle in her left hand. Player two holds his left rope handle in his left hand and player one's left rope handle in his right hand. Players turn at the same time or in opposite time. See the photo.

Questions for Understanding

- Which leg is easier for you to lead with?
- How can you build strength and coordination in your weaker leg?
- How does moving forward in a light jog change your jump rope experience?

KANGAROOS AND PENGUINS

Objective

To tag a partner

Specific Skill Focus

Hopping and shuffling with a ball between the knees

Equipment

One soft ball per player and four cones; soft balls for this activity can be found at dollar stores (pool noodles and sponges also work); Bender Balls can be found at www.benderball.net

Setup

- Mark off a playing area with cones.
- The players put the ball between their knees and squeeze to hold it there.
- Each player finds a partner, and they decide who will be "It" first.
- The leader will call out how each player should move: Kangaroos hop and penguins waddle.

How to Play

- The leader calls out, "Kangaroos," and the players hop like kangaroos. The It begins chasing his partner until he tags her, at which point the tagged player hops on the spot five times and then tries to tag her partner.
- If a player drops his ball, he simply retrieves it and continues play.
- After a short time, the leader calls out, "Penguins." All the players waddle like penguins, and the chasing continues.

Variations

- Vary the starting distance between the partners.
- Instead of five hops, switch to some other exercise such as five burpees or five skips on the spot.
- Vary the size of the playing field.

Questions for Understanding

- How can you use other players to protect yourself from being tagged?
- Where does your movement come from when you are a penguin?
- Where does your power come from when you are a kangaroo?
- How can you avoid losing your ball?

LADDERS

Objective

To quickly move through a ladder outline with predefined movements and patterns

Specific Skill Focus

Fitness and agility

Equipment

A ladder drawn on pavement with chalk or outlined on a floor with tape; each square should be about 1.5 feet (45 cm) across

Setup

A player stands at the beginning of the ladder.

A ladder drawn on pavement with chalk or an actual ladder flat on the ground can be used.

How to Play

- On the signal to begin, or at the start of certain music, the player begins to move from one end of the ladder to the other end with a certain movement and pattern expectation.
- Movement challenges might include running, hopping on one foot (alternating the foot each time through), hopping on two feet, galloping, and sidestepping.
- Patterns might include going straight down the ladder from one end to the other; moving forward two squares and then back one; skipping one square each time; starting at the left side of the first square, moving into the first square, moving to the right side of the first square, moving forward one step, moving to the left of the second square, and so on.
- Have players repeat the activity the desired number of times by running back along the side of the ladder and starting again at the beginning.

1.5 ft (45 cm)

Variations

- Add equipment to the challenge such as dribbling a soccer ball and alternating each foot on top of the ball in each new space, or bouncing a basketball as the player moves through the squares.
- Add music and have students move to the beat of the song—be sure to select a song with a strong beat (see chapter 7 for some suggestions for choosing music).

Questions for Understanding

- What different patterns best suit different sport activities?
- How many different patterns can you make?

PASSING THREES

Objective

To count how many consecutive passes three players can make in 2 minutes

Specific Skill Focus

General warm-up or specifically for volleyball, basketball, soccer, hockey, or football (handoffs)

Equipment

One ball per three players and two cones

Setup

- Position the two cones nine steps apart.
- One player stands at one cone; the other two stand at the other cone, and the first player holds the ball.

How to Play

- On the signal to begin, the first player sets (volleyball) or passes (you can specify the type of pass for basketball, soccer, hockey, or football) the ball to the single player.
- The passer then follows her set or pass and runs to her right around the far cone and awaits a pass.
- The receiver of the pass (you can also specify the type of trap when doing soccer) sets or passes the ball and does the same.
- Play for 2 minutes, and see how many consecutive passes are made without a missed set or pass.

Variation

In football, do the same but practice a handoff, or have players toss the ball on the ground and the receiver does a fumble recovery and then drops the ball for the next player.

Questions for Understanding

- What are key considerations for ensuring the most consecutive passes—not missing any of the sets or passes?
- How can players speed up or slow down this game?

Adapted, by permission, from J. Byl, 2004, *101 fun warm-up and cool-down games* (Champaign, IL: Human Kinetics), 168-169.

ROCK, PAPER, SCISSORS CHASE

Objective

To gather the most points by tagging or avoiding a tag

Specific Skill Focus

Running, changing direction, and tagging

Equipment

Two lines of cones

Setup

- Set up two lines of cones about 10 steps apart.
- Partners face each other in the middle between the two lines.
- Review the game rock, paper, scissors, emphasizing that rock crushes scissors, scissors cut paper, and paper covers rock.

How to Play

- The players say, "Rock, paper, scissors" and finish with their hand signal of choice.
- The winner chases the loser to her cone line, attempting to tag the runner before she reaches her line.
- If the tagger is successful, he scores one point.
- If the runner reaches the cone line without being tagged, she scores a point.
- The two players immediately return to the center and proceed again, and the game continues until one player achieves five points.

Variations

- Rather than keep score, each time a player is tagged, he performs 10 jumping jacks while the tagger counts.
- Sport variations: Both players dribble a soccer ball, basketball, or hockey puck while running.

- Place a pool noodle or sponge on the ground between the two players. The rock, paper, scissors winner must pick up the noodle or sponge and tag the other player with the noodle or thrown sponge to score a point.
- True or False: One side runs away when the answer to a question is true, and the other side runs away when the answer is false—a great way to review material from any class.

Questions for Understanding

- How can you change your starting body position to allow for a faster takeoff?
- Why is it unsafe to run backward?

RUNNING CIRCLES

Objective

To run around a circle and tag the player in front

Specific Skill Focus

General warm-up or specifically for basketball, soccer, lacrosse, or hockey

Equipment

Four cones and three pool noodles

Setup

- Position the four cones four steps apart in a square formation.
- Two players stand opposite each other outside the cones; one player stands in the middle of the cones.
- Each player holds a pool noodle.

How to Play

- On the signal to begin, each player runs around the cones in a counterclockwise circle and tries to tag the other player in front of her with the pool noodle.
- When a player is tagged, the tagged player goes into the middle of the cones and the player in the middle moves outside to stand opposite the remaining runner; these two players now chase each other.
- After a minute or two, switch directions so the players do not get dizzy.

Variation

While players are running around the circle, they dribble a basketball, soccer ball, or hockey ball or puck.

Questions for Understanding

- What are key considerations in controlling the dribbles when running hard around the cones?
- What path around the square corners is the most efficient route when running fast?

SHUTTLE RUN WITH BLOCKS

Objective

To obtain the fastest time running the shuttle course

Specific Skill Focus

Running, changing direction, coordination

Equipment

Wooden blocks or beanbags or sponges (two per player) and a timing device (If you want to make your own beanbags, you can use old fabric. Cut two 7-inch (18 cm) squares and sew three and a half sides. Turn the bag inside out and fill it with dried beans, and then sew the hole shut.)

Setup

- Draw a start line and another line with 10 steps between them.
- Place two blocks on the far line.
- The players line up at the start line.

How to Play

- The first player runs to the far line, picks up one block, runs back to the start line, and places the block on the ground.
- The player then runs to the far line again, picks up the last block, and returns to the start, running through the line.
- The leader can record the time in seconds, or the group can run together in a race, or the group can run a cooperative drill by adding all the players' times together.

Variations

- Add challenges to slow the runners down (e.g., having them hop on one foot or two feet).
- Use different sports equipment instead of blocks.

Questions for Understanding

- How can your footwear affect your running time?
- What helps in speeding up the block pickup or placement?

SPLIT TRIANGLE RUN

Objective

To complete one lap of the field (or more if desired)

Specific Skill Focus

General warm-up or used specifically for basketball, soccer, hockey, football, baseball, volleyball, or badminton (instead of passing a ball, bounce a shuttle on a racket while doing this game)

Equipment

One ball, racket and shuttle, or hockey stick and ball per group

Setup

Three players stand in a triangle formation approximately five steps apart. Player 1 (P1) has a soccer ball.

How to Play

- P1 passes the ball to P2 and then runs between P2 and P3.
- P2 passes the ball to P3 and then runs between P3 and P1.
- P3 passes the ball to P1 and then runs between P1 and P2.
- They repeat the sequence until the group has traveled once around the field.
- Players can never be farther than five steps from each other.

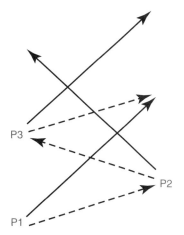

Variation

Thrown-In Split Triangle Run: In this variation, players make a free throw instead of a pass. Players should be around 10 steps apart for this activity. Receiving players should trap the ball, not catch it with their hands.

Questions for Understanding

- What is the most accurate way to pass the ball?
- If a receiver is not quite in position, where should the thrower toss the ball?

Adapted, by permission, from J. Byl, 2004, *101 fun warm-up and cool-down games* (Champaign, IL: Human Kinetics), 147.

SUBTRACT A JACK

Objective

To successfully perform a decreasing number of jumping jacks

Specific Skill Focus

Running, jumping jacks

Equipment

10 cones

Setup

- Set up two rows of cones, about six steps apart.
- Players line up behind one row of cones.

How to Play

- At a signal from the leader, the players perform 10 jumping jacks each. As soon as they are done, they sprint to the opposite cone line and perform 9 jumping jacks.
- Players continue decreasing by 1 jumping jack each side until the last time, when they perform only 1 jumping jack.

Variations

- Change the starting number of cones and jumping jacks.
- Change the method of movement from one side to the other; instead of sprinting, players could hop on one or two feet, or they could perform walking lunges.
- Change the activity at the cone lines from jumping jacks to burpees or push-ups.

Questions for Understanding

- Is it easier to count your moves quietly or out loud?
- What happens to the quality of the exercise (i.e., jumping jacks) when you take your time or when you go very fast?

TABATA DRILLS

Objective

To complete a series of intense moves in a set time at an anaerobic level

Specific Skill Focus

Jumping, rest

Equipment

Watch with a second hand

Setup

Players warm up for 5 minutes by jumping rope, jogging lightly, or cycling.

How to Play

- At a signal from the leader, the players begin a repetitive move, such as jumps with heels kicking together.
- The players repeat this move, jumping as high as possible each time, for 20 seconds.
- The leader then signals for 10 seconds of rest.
- This cycle is repeated seven more times for a total of 4 minutes.
- Follow this 4-minute drill with a 5-minute cool-down.

Variation

Change the jumps to hands touching the heels to lunge switches (start in lunge position; jump up and switch legs), jumping rope at high speed, bench steps, burpees, curb jump-ups, or tuck jumps.

Questions for Understanding

- How can you help calm your breathing during the 10-second rest periods?
- How can you help absorb the landing impact from the jump?
- How can your arms help you jump higher?

Note: The Tabata Protocol is named after Izumi Tabata, PhD, a former researcher at Japan's National Institute of Fitness and Sports in Kanoya, Japan.

TAIL BALL

Objective

To learn different ways of catching a ball with a tail

Specific Skill Focus

General warm-up

Equipment

One leg of a nylon stocking with a tennis ball placed inside the toe of the stocking for each player

Setup

Each player holds a stocking by the tail in an outside area with lots of room in the air above the player.

How to Play

The players swing the ball into the air and count how many different ways they can catch the ball before it hits the ground. For example: Catch the ball, catch the tail, do one push-up and then catch the tail, and so on.

Variation

Have players toss the ball to each other, and each player needs to try to catch the object in a new way each time. See who can successfully catch the ball in the most different ways.

Questions for Understanding

- How does increasing the height of the throw increase or decrease the difficulty of catching the object?
- Is it easier to catch the ball or the tail? Why?

ALLIGATORS

Objective

To move across a set distance while performing modified burpees, or "alligators"

Specific Skill Focus

Power and flexibility

Equipment

None

Setup

- Create a start and finish line about three steps apart.
- All players stand behind the start line facing the finishing line.

How to Play

- At a signal from the leader, the player reaches forward with both hands until they touch the ground. The player then jumps both feet back and completes one push-up.
- Once the push-up is complete, the player jumps both feet forward between her hands and then jumps up into the air, finishing in a standing position.
- The player continues to move forward using this move until she reaches the other side.

Variation

This move can be modified for players with less strength. Instead of jumping both legs back, the player can walk the legs back, and instead of a toe push-up, the player can go down onto the knees for a modified push-up. Instead of jumping the feet forward, the player can walk the feet forward. Players with limited flexibility may be unable to bring their feet to their hands and may need to step forward each time they complete one alligator.

Questions for Understanding

- How can you use your core muscles to help your push-up?
- How can you add power to your jump phase?

BENCH PUSH-UPS AND TRICEPS DIPS

Objective

To successfully perform a set of push-ups and triceps dips on a bench

Specific Skill Focus

Strength

Equipment

A park bench

Setup

The player faces the park bench with feet together.

How to Play

- The player reaches forward with both hands and grabs the edge of the bench.
- The player then walks his feet away from the bench until his arms are straight under his shoulders and his body is flat, like a plank.
- The player then bends his arms, lowers his chest down to the bench, and presses his body back up again.
- After eight push-ups, the player changes position and sits on the bench.
- The player scoots forward on the bench and places the hands on the edge of the bench beside his bottom.
- The heels are on the ground and the knees are bent (easier) or the legs are straight (harder).
- The player then bends at the elbows and allows his body to dip down in front of the bench; he then straightens his arms, raising his body up again.

Use available raised surfaces for triceps dips and for making push-ups more challenging.

Variations

- If indoors, substitute a chair or low table for the park bench. Add this drill to the end of a running drill.
- To make the push-ups more difficult, place the hands on the ground and the toes on the bench. Now do a push-up.

Questions for Understanding

- How does tightening your abdominals change your push-ups?
- Can you control your breathing during both sets of exercises to make them more effective?

MEDICINE BALL PASS

Objective

To pass a medicine ball to a partner

Specific Skill Focus

Core strength, spinal rotation, flexion and extension

Equipment

One medicine ball for each pair of players

Setup

Players stand back to back, and one player holds the medicine ball in front of her body.

How to Play

- The player with the medicine ball rotates her torso to the right and passes the ball to the second player, who has rotated his torso to the left to meet her hands.
- The second player straightens his body and then rotates to the right to continue passing the ball around.
- After 10 rotations, reverse direction. For the second set, the players pass the ball between their legs (under) and above their heads (over).
- After 10 times, reverse the passing direction.

Variations

- Use a basketball or soccer ball instead of a medicine ball.
- Add more players to the pair, and have them stand in a circle for the side pass and in a straight line for the under–over pass.

Questions for Understanding

- How do your core muscles assist your arm and shoulder muscles?
- How can you use your breath to help?
- Are your leg muscles loose or engaged? What works best?

Passing the medicine ball right to left, under, and over.

PLANK HOLDS

Objective

To hold the body in a plank position

Specific Skill Focus

Strength and balance

Equipment

Timing device

Setup

The player joins hands and rests her forearms on the ground, making a triangle of support with the hands and elbows. The player rests her body on the ground.

How to Play

- When the timer begins, the player lifts her body into a balance position using the triangle of support and either her knees (easier) or toes (harder).
- She brings her bottom down into alignment with the rest of her body, forming a straight line, or plank, from the top of her head to her knees (or toes).
- She holds this position for as long as she can and records her time so that next time she can try to beat it.

Variations

- The player can begin in the harder position (toes) and then when tired go into the easier position (knees) until fatigue forces her to stop.
- The move can be changed into a side plank if the player lies on one side and balances on one elbow (placed directly under the shoulder) and the knees or toes.

Be sure to hold body straight when performing any planks.

Questions for Understanding

- Which muscle group is working the hardest during the plank?
- How can your breathing deepen the abdominal work?
- When does the shaking happen? Why is that happening?

UP AND DOWN

Objective

To complete a set number of drills in the shortest amount of time

Specific Skill Focus

Getting up off the ground

Equipment

Timing device

Setup

- All players find an open grassy space.
- The leader sets the timer for 1 minute or 30 seconds.

How to Play

- At the signal to begin, all players lie down on their backs and then roll over onto their abdomens and jump up to a standing position.
- The players repeat this sequence as quickly as possible, counting the number of jumps until the timer goes off.

Variations

- Add a jump off the ground to the standing position.
- Have players roll twice before jumping up.
- Instead of rolling over onto the abdomen, players can roll over into a plank hold for 5 seconds before standing.

Questions for Understanding

- How does tightening your core muscles affect your control?
- How can you soften your landing when you jump?
- If you want to improve your time, is it better to spend more time on your strengths or weaknesses?

CHAPTER

3

TARGET GAMES

We do not quit playing because we grow old,
we grow old because we quit playing.

Oliver Wendell Holmes

Accurately and efficiently hitting a target is important in many games and is the focus of this chapter. Players will learn to hit targets through games involving throwing, rolling, shooting, kicking, and football passing.

There are several different components to accurately hitting a target. Aiming is central, and so is visualization of the object hitting the target; therefore selecting the target to view (or another target closer or farther away) is critical for success. The distance to the intended target and any obstacles between the player and the target must be considered. Positioning is also important, such as positioning of the throwing and nonthrowing arms and feet and positioning of the body relative to the target. The biomechanics of the throw or roll should be executed with the most efficient movement pattern. The skill should be evaluated so adjustments can be made to improve future aim and accuracy.

DISC ARCHERY

Objective

To score as many points as possible by landing a disc close to the middle of a target

Specific Skill Focus

Throwing (soccer, disc, hockey, badminton)

Equipment

One garbage can, one disc, chalk or rope to mark two other circles, and a timing device

Setup

- Place a garbage can in the playing area. If using chalk, draw a circle around the garbage can (garbage can is the center of the circle) with about a 4-step radius, and then draw another circle with an 8-step radius.
- Draw a tossing line about 10 steps from the garbage can.

How to Play

- Determine how long the game will last—usually 1 or 2 minutes is plenty.
- At the signal from the timer to begin, the player (standing behind the tossing line) throws the disc at the garbage can.
- Scoring is as follows: In the garbage can is worth eight points, hitting the garbage can is worth six points, landing on the first circle is worth four points, landing on the second circle is worth two points, and landing outside the second circle is worth one point.
- After throwing the disc, the player runs to retrieve the disc and count the points. The player then runs back to the tossing line and does another throw. This process continues until time runs out.
- This is a great mental math activity as well.

Variations

- Give the tosser several discs, and have one or two people retrieve the discs so the tosser can focus only on completing the most accurate tosses.
- For more skilled players, increase the distance the tossing line is from the target; for less skilled players, move the tossing line closer.

Questions for Understanding

- What are some strategies to ensure accuracy when pressured by time?
- How does the height of the toss make a difference in terms of accuracy?

DISC GOLF

Objective

To score as low a score as possible by hitting the targets in as few throws as possible

Specific Skill Focus

Throwing (bowling, soccer, disc, football, lacrosse, hockey, badminton, baseball)

Equipment

One disc (or any kind of ball—even a soccer ball that is kicked) per player; natural objects such as trees or equipment such as cones or hoops

Setup

- Set up nine targets (for younger children, the targets might be only about 10 steps away; for older children the distances can be increased by 10 times—probably best played on a larger field).
- The targets could be natural targets such as trees, posts, and parts of buildings, or they could be cones or hoops with numbered flags or labels on them.

How to Play

- A player begins at a starting line.
- The player throws her disc toward the first target and throws again until the target is hit.
- Players keep track of their scores (each throw counts 1) by adding in their heads—good mental mathematics development.
- When the first target is hit, the player then throws her disc toward the next target.

Variation

Speed Golf—Players try to time how quickly they can make their throws (or kicks), hit each target in order, and complete the entire course—players must hit each target in five throws or fewer or 10 seconds is added as a penalty per extra throw. Speed Golf makes for a great warm-up.

Questions for Understanding

- How does one gain both the greatest distance and accuracy?
- Is it easier to stand directly facing the target or standing sideways to the target? Why?

DOUBLE DISC COURT

Objective

To get the other team to be holding both discs or balls or birdies

Specific Skill Focus

Catching, running, and throwing (soccer, disc, football, lacrosse, badminton)

Equipment

Two discs or balls or birdies and racquets and eight or more markers to mark two courts

Setup

- Officially, the courts are 13-step squares that are 17 steps apart from each other. For children, you will need smaller-sized courts that are closer together, something like 5-step squares that are 5 to 10 steps apart—mark these with the cones or other markers.
- Position one player, or teams of two players, in each court (when playing with two players, the two players must take turns catching and throwing the disc).
- One player in each court holds a disc.

How to Play

- When the two teams are ready to serve the servers call out, "Ready, two, one, throw." On "throw" they throw the disc into the opponent's court. After the first serve, players have 3 seconds to get ready to make their return throw—no need to wait for the other team to get ready.
- If the disc lands outside the court, then the game stops and the other team scores a point.
- If a disc is dropped by someone, then the game stops and the other team scores a point.
- If a disc lands in a court without being touched, then the throwing team scores a point.
- If a team is holding both discs, then the game stops and the other team scores two points.

Questions for Understanding

- How can you make one disc take a long time to land in a court and then make the next disc get to that court quickly?
- How do you know where to go to catch the disc or ball?

For more detailed rules, go to www.wfdf.org/index.php?page=rules/art2.htm.

NAILING IT

Objective

To throw as accurately as possible

Specific Skill Focus

Throwing (soccer, basketball, disc, football, lacrosse, hockey, badminton, tennis, volleyball, baseball)

Equipment

A plastic disc and a target on the ground that is a one-and-a-half-step square drawn with chalk or laid out with ropes; a large plastic hoop also works

Setup

Set up the target and establish a throwing line.

How to Play

- A player throws the disc at the target.
- If the player is successful, she takes three large steps backward and tries again.
- If the player is unsuccessful, she takes one large step forward and tries again.
- Have another player return the disc, or the player could retrieve her own disc and use a marker to identify the spot the next throw is to be taken from.

Variations

Use balls instead of discs. It may be easier to roll the balls into the target if you want them to stay in the target—rolling the balls into a plastic hoop makes this easier.

Questions for Understanding

- What are the keys to throwing accurately?
- How does distance affect accuracy?

FIVE-PIN BLASTER

Objective

To knock down all five pins with three balls or fewer, achieving the highest score

Specific Skill Focus

Kicking, rolling, and throwing (bowling, soccer, basketball, disc, football, lacrosse, hockey, badminton, tennis, volleyball, baseball)

Equipment

Five empty two-liter plastic soda bottles, cleaned and filled with water, or full water bottles; an empty indoor space with smooth flooring, such as hardwood or linoleum, or an outdoor space with pavement; and a ball that can be gripped with one hand

Setup

- Set up the five plastic bottles side by side at the far end of a space. For younger players, an alley distance of five steps is sufficient; older players can be challenged with a longer distance. Mark off a line that the players must stand behind when rolling the ball.
- Attach value stickers to each bottle: five points for the middle one, three for the next-to-center bottles, and two each for the end bottles.

How to Play

- The player grasps her first ball and stands a few steps behind the line.
- She takes a few steps forward, bringing the ball hand behind her side, and as she stops at the line, she releases the ball low to the ground so that it rolls toward the pins.
- She has three throws in a turn, and then all the points are added up.

Variations

- Change the amount of water in the plastic bottles to make them heavier or lighter. Change the ball to a heavier or lighter ball.
- Allow the player to throw the ball with two hands from between the legs. Introduce proper scoring to account for spares and strikes.
- Set up a score sheet with up to 10 frames to have a full bowling game.

Questions for Understanding

- How does the amount of water in the plastic bottles affect the difficulty of the game?
- How does the weight of the ball change the game?
- What happens to your roll if you roll the ball while your feet are beside each other instead of one behind the other (a walking position)?

LONG ACCURACY ROLLS

Objective

To determine how far away from each other two players can get and still roll accurately

Specific Skill Focus

Rolling (bowling, soccer)

Equipment

One ball for each pair of players

Setup

Two players stand opposite each other, approximately 10 steps apart. One player holds the ball.

How to Play

- The first player rolls the ball so that it goes between the other player's outstretched legs.
- If successful, then the bowler takes three steps backward.
- Now the other player rolls the ball.
- If a player misses rolling the ball between the legs, then the bowler moves forward two steps.
- Players see how far away from each other they can get.

Variations

Hill Rolls: Do the same activity but with two players standing along a hill. The ball will need to be rolled along and up the hill to roll down to the receiving player.

Questions for Understanding

- How can you improve accuracy with increasing distance?
- Where is it best to look when rolling the ball to a target?

MISS THE PINS

Objective

To miss the pins while bowling, achieving the lowest score

Specific Skill Focus

Rolling (bowling)

Equipment

Five empty two-liter plastic soda or water bottles; an empty indoor space with smooth flooring, such as hardwood or linoleum, or an outdoor space with pavement; and a ball that can be gripped with one hand.

Setup

- Set up the five plastic bottles side by side (at least one-and-a-half ball widths apart) at the far end of the space. For younger players, an alley distance of five steps is sufficient; older players can be challenged with a longer distance. Mark off a line that the players must stand behind when rolling the ball.
- Attach value stickers to each bottle: five points for the middle one, three for the next-to- center bottles, and two each for the end bottles.

How to Play

- The player rolls the ball from behind the line and between the two outside pins, trying to roll the ball through the pins without hitting any. If a pin is knocked down it is removed, making it easier to roll a ball through the pins without knocking others down.
- The player must roll three balls in a turn.
- Any ball rolled outside of the two outside pins must be redone. Add the scores of the fallen pins. The goal is to score as few points as possible.

Variation

Set up a full bowling game with 10 frames, and count the points to see which player has the lowest score.

Questions for Understanding

- Which is more difficult: aiming to hit the pins or aiming to miss the pins?
- Where is it best to look when rolling for open spaces?

TEN-PIN SLAM

Objective

To knock down as many pins as possible with three balls, achieving the highest score

Specific Skill Focus

Rolling (bowling)

Equipment

10 empty aluminum soda or juice cans, drained and dried, and three tennis balls

Setup

- Set up the 10 pins in any formation the players agree upon.
- Mark off an alley on a smooth floor space or an outdoor paved space.
- Mark off a line the players must stand behind when rolling the ball.

Look at the cans while rolling the ball in Ten-Pin Slam.

How to Play

- The player chooses his ball and stands a few steps back from the line, facing the pins.
- He then takes a few steps forward and rolls the ball at the line toward the pins.
- After three rolls, the points are counted up, assigning one point per pin.

Variations

- Change the formation of the pins, angling them out from the first pin.
- Introduce scoring using strikes and spares.
- Set up a score sheet with up to 15 frames.
- In warm weather, use a water-filled balloon outdoors to roll or throw at the pins.

Questions for Understanding

- How does the pin setup affect how many pins get knocked down?
- Can you use some fallen pins to help knock down other pins?
- What happens to the effectiveness of your throws if your ball bounces instead of rolls?

TWO-PLAYER BOWLING

Objective

To try to score points by bowling or kicking a ball as close as possible to a target

Specific Skill Focus

Rolling and kicking (bowling, soccer)

Equipment

One ball for each pair of players

Setup

- Two players stand a predetermined distance apart.
- The bowler holds the ball.
- The other player spreads her feet two ball widths apart.

How to Play

- The bowler rolls a ball toward the target player.
- If the ball goes through the legs without hitting either leg, then the bowler scores three points.
- If the ball hits one of the legs, then the bowler scores two points.
- If the ball goes outside the legs without hitting either leg, then the bowler scores one point.
- From the position he was in, the bowler now becomes a target, and the target is the new bowler.
- Bowl 10 times and see how many points each bowler can get.

Variation

Players stand facing each other 10 steps apart, with legs shoulder-width apart. They take turns kicking the ball and trying to have it go between the opponent's legs. Each successful kick counts for one point.

Questions for Understanding

- How can you increase the success of your bowling?
- How can this game be made easier or harder?
- What is the most accurate way to roll or kick the ball?

HE SHOOTS, HE SCORES

Objective

To score a goal with each shot

Specific Skill Focus

Kicking and throwing (soccer, lacrosse, hockey)

Equipment

One soccer ball (or lacrosse stick and ball or hockey stick and puck or ball)

Setup

- Set up a goal with a goalie (you could also have an empty net or put a box or two in the net or a blue recycling bin; the recycling bin, "Mr. Blue," cannot be hit).
- The striker is at the edge of the penalty area, or 10 to 20 steps away.

How to Play

- Pass a ball to the striker's foot, lacrosse player's stick, or pass the puck to the hockey player's stick. She one-times her kick against the goal—this means no trapping or dribbling, just an immediate kick.
- Count how many goals were scored after 10 tries.

Variation

- Instead of rolling the balls, bounce the ball to the striker and allow the striker to trap (catch) the ball or puck and then shoot.
- Have a shooter on either side of the goal, and have a leader at the goal line feeding the balls. This way there is always someone to retrieve the ball (or puck) when it goes through the goal.

Questions for Understanding

- How does a striker improve goal-scoring effectiveness?
- How does a goalie most effectively prevent the striker from scoring?

HOPSCOTCH POTSY

Objective

To hop from square one to the finish without stepping out of the boxes

Specific Skill Focus

Throwing, catching, hopping, and jumping

Equipment

Chalk and a small stone

Setup

- Draw a hopscotch pattern on the ground, making a line of boxes (see figure).
- Number each box sequentially.

How to Play

- The player stands behind the first box and throws a stone onto box one.
- He then hops over number one, lands on two, and then continues to hop into each box in order to the finish.
- The player then turns around and hops in all the boxes, stopping at box two, and bends over to pick up the stone.
- If no errors are made, the player throws again, this time onto box two, and repeats the sequence; he then tosses into box three, then four, and so on.
- If the marker does not land in the appropriate box, the player tries again.
- If there is a marker on either box three or four or six and seven, the player lands with one foot in the box beside it (not with both feet as in previous times when there was no marker in either box. For example, if the marker is in box three, the player would balance on one foot in box four, which is beside it.

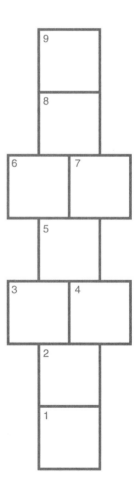

Variations

- The number of boxes can be varied to suit the age and ability of the player.
- The shape of the hopscotch pattern can be changed to a circular, linear, snakelike, or snail pattern.
- When played with two or three players, when a player throws a marker and misses the correct box, the marker is returned to the box the marker was last in, and the next player attempts to land his marker in his box and then hop through the course.

Question for Understanding

- How can you change your body position to allow you to bend over on one foot without falling?
- Is it harder to skip on one foot than the other? Can you change feet?

LONG ACCURACY THROWS

Objective

To determine how far away from each other two players can get and still throw (or kick) accurately

Specific Skill Focus

Catching, overhand throwing, and throwing (soccer, basketball, disc, football, lacrosse, hockey, baseball)

Equipment

One ball (and each player has a baseball glove or lacrosse stick depending on the sport) for each pair of players

Setup

Two players stand opposite each other, approximately 10 steps apart. One player holds the ball.

How to Play

- The first player throws the ball so the other player can catch it without moving either foot.
- If successful, then the throwing player takes three steps backward.
- Now the other player throws the ball. If a player misses the ball, then the thrower moves forward two steps.

Variation

Over Accurate: Have the players throw or kick the ball over an obstacle (e.g., a fence, swing set, or tree).

Questions for Understanding

- How can you improve accuracy with increasing distance?
- What makes it easier to catch or trap the ball?

SOCCER BILLIARDS

Objective

To kick a ball against another ball and have the other ball go through a target

Specific Skill Focus

Kicking (soccer)

Equipment

Six cones, three different-colored balls, and one soccer ball

Setup

- Have three goals (each about one step wide) marked with cones or other objects placed in a triangle (maybe five steps long).
- Position three different-colored balls (identify one as the eight ball—which has to go in last) in the center of the triangle.

How to Play

- From outside the triangle, the first player kicks a soccer ball against the other three balls.
- Players then take turns trying to kick the soccer ball against one of the other balls and have it go into one of the goals (if the soccer ball goes into a goal at the same time, then the other ball is returned to the center of the triangle).
- When a player scores, she gets to play again.
- Any time the soccer ball goes outside the triangle, the next player can place the ball anywhere along the edge of the triangle.
- When a player gets one ball in, he tries to score a goal by bumping the eight-ball into a goal.
- When both players have scored with their balls, then both are trying to score with the eight-ball.

Variation

Players roll the ball instead of kicking it.

Questions for Understanding

- What are effective ways to figure out the best place to hit the ball?
- How can you hit the center balls to make it harder for the other players to score?

THREE IN A ROW

Objective

To throw accurately enough to get three beanbags in a row on a tic-tac-toe target

Specific Skill Focus

Throwing (baseball)

Equipment

10 beanbags or stuffed animals per pair of players (half should be a different color from the other half)

Setup

Design a tic-tac-toe board by taping lines on the floor with masking tape or using chalk on pavement. Squares should be about one shoe length in width—make the targets bigger if you want the students to throw from farther away.

How to Play

- The players take turns throwing their objects onto the tic-tac-toe board.
- The first player to get her objects to land on three squares forming a line across the board is the winner.
- Two objects from different players can be on the same square. If one player gets two of his objects on one square, he can remove one of the objects and use it on a subsequent turn.
- When all the objects have been thrown, players collect their objects that are not on the board.

Variations

- If a player is the first to land an object on a square, the other player cannot land and keep her object on the same square.
- If two players are competing and one is older, challenge the older player to use a more difficult way of tossing the object (e.g., standing on one foot when tossing, standing farther away).

Questions for Understanding

- How can you increase or decrease the difficulty of this game?
- How does the shape of the object affect the final landing?

TIMED BALL KICKS

Objective

To achieve the highest number of accurate hits on a target in 1 minute

Specific Skill Focus

Kicking and throwing (soccer, basketball, lacrosse, hockey)

Equipment

One soccer ball, basketball, or lacrosse ball and stick and one wall target per player (either painted, chalked, or attached) and a timing device

Setup

Each player faces his target on the wall, ready to kick his soccer ball or throw his ball, and the timer gets ready to time 1 minute.

How to Play

- The players kick or throw the ball, aiming for the target.
- Each time the ball bounces back, they kick or throw it again, counting the number of hits on the target.
- When the timer indicates that 1 minute has passed, the players remember their number and prepare to try again in an effort to improve their score.

Variations

- If you have space for only one target, you can have one player go at a time, while the other players cheer and help count.
- To vary this activity further, have the players count continuous target hits, starting over each time they miss the target.
- You can also have the students work in teams of two, alternating kicks or throws between the two players.
- To change the scoring, use a dartboard-style target, with varying points in different sections.

Questions for Understanding

- How can you increase the number of contacts in 1 minute?
- Where is the most helpful place to look when kicking or throwing or catching a rebound?
- In basketball, can you use your wrist flick to get a sharper shot?
- Can you engage your abdominals to get more power?

TIMED WALL DRIBBLE

Objective

To dribble and pass the ball as many times as possible in 1 minute

Specific Skill Focus

Catching, dribbling, overhand throwing, and throwing (basketball, lacrosse, hockey)

Equipment

One ball and one wall target per player (either painted, chalked, or attached), one dribbling spot 10 steps from the wall, one passing spot about 5 steps from the wall, and one timer

Setup

Each player faces the target on the wall at the dribbling spot and holds a ball. A passing line is drawn on the ground halfway between the dribbling spot and the wall.

Take aim and shoot.

How to Play

- The player dribbles the ball to the passing spot and then passes the ball to the target, attempting to hit the target's center.
- When the ball bounces back, the player gains control of the ball with one hand and immediately dribbles back to the dribbling spot. He repeats the cycle.

Target

Passing line

- Players count how many times they can hit the target in 1 minute.

Dribbling spot

Variations

- To make this drill easier, the player can catch the rebound with two hands before beginning to dribble.
- To make it harder, the player must execute a full turn after passing and before catching the rebound.
- Two players can use the same target with two balls, or two players can share a target and a ball, taking turns with the ball.

Questions for Understanding

- Where do you look when you are passing to the target?
- What body position makes it easiest for you to prepare to receive the rebounding ball?

WALLING FOR DISTANCE

Objective

To determine how far away from the wall a player can get and still hit the target

Specific Skill Focus

Throwing (soccer, basketball, disc, football, lacrosse, hockey, baseball)

Equipment

One ball, one large wall target (either painted, chalked, or attached), and one cone or marker per player

Setup

Each player faces her target on the wall from about 10 steps away and puts her marker there.

How to Play

- The players throw the ball so it hits the target.
- If successful, the player takes five steps backward, puts her marker on the new spot, and tries to hit the target again. If successful, the player takes another five steps backward, and if unsuccessful then the player moves forward five steps.

Variations

- Two players pass the ball to each other.
- One player is the target and can pivot on either foot to catch the ball, but if the ball is farther away than that, the thrower must move up for the next throw.
- After 10 throws, switch the thrower and target players.

Questions for Understanding

- How can you improve your accuracy?
- How does following through (finishing the movement forward after the ball is released or kicked) affect your ability to hit the target?

HUT

Objectives

Warming up and practicing long snaps

Specific Skill Focus

Throwing (football)

Equipment

Four markers and one football per group

Setup

Make a square four steps across; players are positioned at three of the corners.

How to Play

- One player snaps the ball and then goes to the open spot.
- The player who receives the snap then snaps it to the next player and moves across to the corner vacated by the previous player.
- Continue to lengthen the distance until the players are about 12 or 13 steps apart.
- If a pass is missed, the players should move closer together.

Variation

Speed Snap: Count how many successful snaps the players can make in 2 minutes.

Questions for Understanding

- What is the easiest way to receive the ball?
- What is the easiest way to snap a spiral?
- How does the height of the throw affect the distance and accuracy?

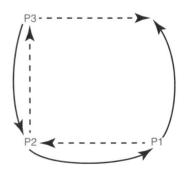

TERRITORY INVASION GAMES

Do you know what my favorite part of the game is?
The opportunity to play.

Mike Singletary

Many games involve invading someone else's territory. Think of games such as soccer or basketball when you need to invade and beat the other team's defense and then score a goal or a basket. The games in this chapter help students learn to invade by teaching them dribbling, ball control, passing, and shooting, and they also learn the flipside of offense: defending your territory.

These territory invasion games are all about maintaining control of the ball with your team, trying to put invasive pressure on the other team by moving the ball into the best scoring opportunity, and then scoring on the target. At the same time, the other team tries to get possession of the ball, prevent the invasive movements, and limit scoring opportunities. In the end, the intention is to score more goals than the opponent and to limit the opponent's score. These are very challenging games because there is continuous action, and players regularly and quickly need to change their roles from playing offense to playing defense.

CARD BOUNCERS

Objective

To dribble and collect as many points as possible in a set amount of time (2 or 3 minutes should be plenty)

Specific Skill Focus

Dribbling and kicking (soccer, basketball, hockey)

Equipment

Basketball or soccer ball for dribbling, or hockey stick and ball or puck for shooting against a wall, or volleyball for serving against the wall at a specific height, plus a deck of playing cards

Setup

- Three steps from the wall, lay a deck of cards facedown and add a restraining line from which the player must kick or serve.
- Eight steps from the wall, position a starting line; this is where the player begins and returns to each time.

How to Play

- On the signal to begin, the player dribbles or stickhandles to the deck of cards and picks one up.
- The player quickly bounces the basketball in one spot, or kicks, shoots, or serves against the wall, the number of times indicated on the card (face cards are worth 10; an ace is worth 1 point).
- When the challenge is finished, the player returns to the start line, deposits the card, and dribbles or stickhandles back to the deck of cards to repeat the challenge.
- When the time is up, the number of points is the total of the numbers on the cards.

Variation

Card Bouncers With Defense: Play this game with two players, one trying to cross the line where the cards are and the other trying to keep this player from advancing.

Questions for Understanding

- How can you dribble more quickly?
- If this game were a race between an older and younger player, how could you change the rules to make the race more fair?

DRIBBLE TAG

Objective
To not have your ball tagged by the It

Specific Skill Focus
Dodging, dribbling, running (soccer and basketball)

Equipment
One ball per player and four cones to define the playing area

Setup
- Set up the cones in a 10-step square.
- Players distribute themselves in the playing area, each with a ball.
- Assign one player to be It.

How to Play
- All players dribble their balls.
- The It dribbles the ball and tries to tag someone else's ball with her hand in the case of basketball and with her feet in the case of soccer. If the It is successful, then the tagged player becomes the new It.

Variation
No-Ball It: The It does not have a ball, which makes it easier for her to tag someone else's ball. When she is successful, the It trades places with the player whose ball she tagged.

Questions for Understanding
- What are some of the best ways to protect your ball?
- What are some of the best ways to tag someone else's ball?

HOG

Objective

For one player to keep the ball from two other players

Specific Skill Focus

Dodging, dribbling, running (soccer and basketball)

Equipment

One ball per three players and four cones to define the playing area

Setup

- Set up the cones in an 8- to 12-step square.
- Give one player the ball.

How to Play

- On the leader's signal, the player with the ball tries to prevent the other two players from getting his ball.
- Meanwhile, the other two players try to get the ball from the dribbler without holding or pushing his body.

Variation

Play two versus two so the dribbler has a teammate to pass to.

Questions for Understanding

- How can you best protect the ball from being taken?
- How can you best take the ball away from a dribbler?

OBSTACLE DRIBBLE

Objective
To improve dribbling skill

Specific Skill Focus
Dodging, dribbling, and running (soccer, basketball, lacrosse, hockey)

Equipment
Cones, plastic hoops, jump ropes, and a timing device

Setup
- Design an age-appropriate obstacle course with the objects you have chosen.
- Set out cones to dribble around, hoops to dribble in, and jump ropes on the ground so that the player can dribble on either side.

Players use ball handling skills to get around objects in Obstacle Dribble.

How to Play

- Have the first player start dribbling the ball at the start cone, and time how long it takes her to get through the whole course.
- Once she is finished, start the next player.
- If players lose the ball, then have them retrieve it and go back to the place where they lost it and continue from there.

Variations

- Send the players through the course in 10-second intervals, forcing them to be aware of other players and balls.
- For able players, add challenge by raising the hoops higher off the ground and having two turners move the jump rope, in a side-to-side swing, a low-to-the-ground snake motion, or a full turn.
- Add a hand challenge by assigning a turn when players must dribble with the left hand only (or the right if they are left-handed).
- Add a control challenge by forcing players who lose balls to go back to the beginning of the course.

Questions for Understanding

- Which hand or foot is easier to dribble with?
- When is it easier to control the ball—while rushing forward or taking your time?

ROBIN'S NEST

Objective

To score the required number of points

Specific Skill Focus

Dodging, dribbling, and running (soccer, basketball)

Equipment

Four plastic hoops and five soccer balls

Setup

- Take the players to an open area outside.
- Place the hoops in a triangle, with another hoop in the center.
- Each hoop should be about three to five steps from the center.
- Place the soccer balls in the center hoop.
- Divide the players behind each hoop. If there are teams of two, have them stand in a line behind one of the hoops around the triangle.

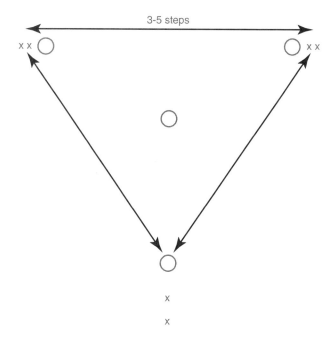

How to Play

- On the leader's signal to begin, each runner runs to the center hoop, picks up a ball, and dribbles it back to his hoop.
- The ball must stay in the hoop. If it rolls out, he goes back and puts it in.
- Once the ball is in the hoop, that player gets another ball. If there are more players per hoop, then the player that just went goes to the back of the line, and the next player runs.
- The players return to the center hoop *or* to another team's hoop to grab another ball.
- Teams cannot prevent other players from taking the ball from their own hoops, but they can shout encouragement and advice (such as where to take a ball from) to their own team members.
- When one player or team has three balls in their hoop, that round is over and that team gets a point.
- This is an excellent sprinting activity. It is a fast-moving game in which at least three players work very hard for a short time, have a short rest, and then are active again.

Questions for Understanding

- What are the most effective ways, and the quickest, of getting the most balls in your hoop?
- How can you kick your ball into your hoop without having it roll out the other side?
- To keep another team from getting three balls, what is important to do?

Adapted, by permission, from CIRA Ontario, 2010, Activities for spaces in and around the building. In *Everybody move!: A multimedia package for daily physical activity*, 2nd ed. (Champaign, IL: Human Kinetics), 78-79.

SLALOM COURSE

Objective

To measure how quickly a player can complete an obstacle course

Specific Skill Focus

Racket familiarization, running (badminton and tennis)

Equipment

One racket and ball or shuttle per player, a series of markers (cones), and a timing device with a second hand

Setup

Establish a start and finish line, and then set up a series of markers (cones) between them.

How to Play

- On the signal to begin, the player dribbles the ball along the ground (or bounces the shuttle on the racket) and around the cones, using the racket to move the ball.
- Measure how quickly a player can accomplish this.

Questions for Understanding

- What can you do to increase both speed and control of the ball?
- Is it more helpful to look ahead at the next cone or to look at your ball?

SLOW DRIBBLER

Objective

To tackle the ball away from a slow dribbler

Specific Skill Focus

Running and slide tackling (soccer)

Equipment

One soccer ball per pair of players

Setup

- Pick a day when the grass is a bit wet from rain or dew.
- Make sure the ground is safe and free from any protruding objects such as rocks or glass.
- One player has a ball about five steps away from another player.

How to Play

- The player with the ball dribbles slowly away from the defender.
- The defender runs to the dribbler and slide-tackles the ball away.

Questions for Understanding

- How do you slide without hurting yourself?
- What are the most effective ways to slide-tackle a ball away from a dribbler?
- How does the speed of your run affect the length of your slide?

SPRINTERS

Objective

To measure how quickly a player can sprint a short distance (50 steps) and keep control of a ball

Specific Skill Focus

Dribbling, running, and stick handling (soccer, basketball, hockey)

Equipment

One ball per player or one hockey stick and ball per player and a timing device

Setup

Determine a start and finish line. It could be the same line, but you will need a line 25 steps away where players switch directions.

How to Play

- On the leader's signal to go, the players try to quickly dribble and run to the finish line (or to the turning line and back).
- The players must not take more than five steps without touching the ball with their feet (or stick or hands).

Variation

Complete this activity as a timed event with only one player going.

Questions for Understanding

- How can you run very fast and keep effective control of the ball?
- How can you plan for a direction change and keep control of the ball?

TIGHT-QUARTER DRIBBLE

Objective

To dribble a ball without losing contact with it

Specific Skill Focus

Dribbling and running (soccer, basketball, hockey)

Equipment

One soccer ball or basketball per player and 40 meters or 40 yards of rope to mark the playing area

Setup

- Mark the outer boundaries of the playing area with the rope.
- Each player has a ball by her feet.

How to Play

- All players must keep close contact with their balls and try to kick away another player's ball. When a player gets her ball kicked away from her and it goes outside the playing area, that player gets a point scored against her.
- Play for several minutes. Whoever has the fewest points is the winner.

Players defend and attack at the same time in Tight-Quarter Dribble.

Variation

Tight-Quarter Dribble With an It: Have one player be It. He also dribbles a ball and tries to kick other players' balls out of the playing area. When a player loses her ball, she becomes the new It.

Questions for Understanding

- How can you best protect your ball from being kicked away?
- How can you best dribble your ball and kick another player's ball away?

WHAT TIME IS IT, MR. WOLF?

Objective
To tag the wall without getting tagged

Specific Skill Focus
Dribbling and running (soccer, basketball, hockey)

Equipment
One ball per player and a smooth area to dribble a ball (basketball) or a grassy area (soccer)

Setup
One player, the Wolf, faces the wall; the other attacking players stand 10 to 20 steps back at a start line, each with a ball.

How to Play
- The attacking players call out, "What time is it, Mr. Wolf?" If Mr. Wolf calls out, "Three o'clock," the players move forward three steps and call out again.
- If an attacking player reaches the wall, then this player becomes the new Mr. Wolf.
- Mr. Wolf can also call out, "Dinnertime." The Wolf dribbles his ball (as do all the other players) and tries to tag a player before the player gets back to the start line.
- If a player is tagged, then that player begins the new game five steps farther back from the start line.

Variation
For younger players, play this game without dribbling a ball.

Questions for Understanding
- How can you dribble a ball with control and be ready to retreat quickly?
- How can you best quickly turn your ball to escape when "dinnertime" is called?

JUGGLERS

Objective

To see how long each player can juggle the ball

Specific Skill Focus

Juggling (soccer)

Equipment

One soccer ball for each player

How to Play

- A player drops a ball to her feet and kicks the ball back up to herself.
- She continues to keep the ball up as long as possible, using any part of her body except her arms and hands.
- For beginning players, allow one bounce on the ground between kicks.
- Kicking the ball with a bit of backspin helps the juggler keep the ball nearby.

Variation

Group Juggle: Instead of a single juggler, two to five jugglers can work together using one ball. The group tries to count how many successive kicks they can perform before the ball lands on the ground. Jugglers can kick the ball to themselves a maximum of three times before passing the ball to another juggler.

Questions for Understanding

- What can you do to increase the number of times you can juggle the ball?
- How can you move your leg and foot to add backspin to the ball?

Adapted, by permission, from J. Byl, 2004, *101 fun warm-up and cool-down games* (Champaign, IL: Human Kinetics), 156.

SPEED TRAP

Objective

To score a goal by kicking the ball past a competitor's trap

Specific Skill Focus

Trapping (soccer)

Equipment

One soccer ball and four cones (to define the goals) for each pair of players

Setup

- Make two goals, 1 step in width and approximately 10 steps apart.
- Players stand in their goals, and one player has a ball.

How to Play

- Each player takes a turn at trying to score a goal by kicking the soccer ball along the ground at the opponent's goal.
  - If the shot is wide, then no point is scored.
  - If the shot is on goal and the defender traps the ball, then no point is scored.
  - If the shot is on goal and goes past the defender, or if the defender fails to trap the ball, then a point is scored.
- Play until 20 points.

Variation

Move the two players farther away from each other, and discuss how that influences the ease or difficulty of trapping a ball.

Questions for Understanding

- What are tips for effectively trapping the ball?
- What is the most helpful direction to face your body when the ball comes in? (Face the ball directly? Angle yourself slightly to one side?)

GRID PASS

Objective

To pass the ball to a partner on an adjacent corner without having the ball intercepted or without being tagged while holding the ball

Specific Skill Focus

Catching, kicking, running, skipping, and throwing (soccer, basketball, disc, football, lacrosse, hockey)

Equipment

One soccer ball and four cones or markers to delineate a square

Setup

Define a square with sides approximately four to six steps long. Three players stand on corners of the grid, and one player stands in the middle.

How to Play

- One player (P1) begins with the ball in one of the grid corners.
- The other two players (P2 and P3) are positioned at adjacent corners, leaving one corner open.
- The player with the ball can pass it only to one of the two adjacent corners (he cannot pass the ball across the grid or dribble the ball).
- Once the pass has been made, the player who did not receive the ball moves to the open corner to give the receiver two corners to pass the ball to.
- The middle player (MP) tries to intercept the ball or force a bad pass or tag the player with the ball.
- Play continues until a player makes a bad pass or the player in the middle intercepts the ball or tags the player with the ball.
- When that happens, the player who made the errant pass or was tagged goes into the middle and is replaced by the MP.

MP

- This game helps players learn to execute accurate passes. Players should use deception and not telegraph whom they intend to pass the ball to. Players without the ball should always go to the open space to ensure the possibility of two receivers.

Questions for Understanding

- How can the offense best avoid being intercepted or tagged while in possession of the ball?
- How can the defense best intercept the ball or tag a player in possession of the ball?

Adapted, by permission, from J. Byl, 2004, *101 fun warm-up and cool-down games* (Champaign, IL: Human Kinetics), 152.

PARTNER PASS

Objective
To pass the ball accurately to a partner while moving down a court

Specific Skill Focus
Catching, dribbling, overhand throwing, running, and throwing (soccer, basketball, disc, football, lacrosse, hockey)

Equipment
One basketball for each pair of players

Setup
Two players face each other, standing 5 feet (1.5 m) apart. One player has the ball.

How to Play
- The player with the ball begins to dribble, and both players start jogging down the court (this could be a parking lot or gym).
- The player with the ball passes the ball to his partner, who catches it, dribbles, and passes back.

Variation
Do only one type of pass each time the players run down the court.

Questions for Understanding
- How can you change your body position to throw with more power?
- Which hand is easier to pass with?
- How can you signal to your partner that you are about to pass?

TWO-TO-ONE KEEP-AWAY

Objective

To count how many times a ball can be passed between two players

Specific Skill Focus

Catching, dodging, dribbling, kicking, overhand throwing, running, and throwing (soccer, basketball, disc, football, lacrosse, hockey)

Equipment

One ball and something to mark off two adjacent squares

Setup

- Mark off one square, about five steps across—if there are more than four players, increase the size of the squares a little.
- Two players form a team and stand in the square in possession of the ball.
- One player from the other team stands inside the square; the other player waits outside the square.

How to Play

- On the leader's signal to begin, the two players with the ball begin to pass the ball to each other, counting each successful pass out loud.
- At the same time, the other player tries to intercept or steal the ball.
- When the interceptor is successful, the interceptor's partner joins her in the square and they try to successfully pass as many balls as they can back and forth, counting each successful pass out loud. One of the first team's players leaves the square (a quick game of rock, paper, scissors can determine who goes out; the winner stays in); the other remains in the square and tries to intercept a pass or steal the ball.
- See which team can score the most consecutive passes.

Questions for Understanding

- How can players most effectively get the most passes to each other?
- How can players most effectively intercept the ball?

DOUBLE CONE BALL

Objective

To score more goals, by kicking the ball against one of the opponent's cones, than the opponent does

Specific Skill Focus

Dodging, dribbling, running, and throwing (soccer, lacrosse, hockey)

Equipment

One soccer ball and four cones for each pair of players

Setup

- Set up two cones three steps apart (like a goal).
- Set up another pair of cones 10 steps away.
- One player begins at each set of cones.

How to Play

- One player begins with the ball and attempts to dribble by her opponent and kick the ball against one of her opponent's cones.
- The other player tries to prevent her from doing so and tries to intercept the ball and kick it against her opponent's cones.
- After a player has scored a goal, the other player gets to dribble the ball three steps from her goal line before her opponent can defend against her.

Variations

- Use just one cone or pin per player or team.
- Play two on two or three on three.
- Instead of hitting the cones to score, the players must kick the ball in between the two cones to score.

Questions for Understanding

- What are the best ways to control the dribble so that the opponent does not get the ball?

- What are the best ways to get past the defense to score?
- What are the best ways to defend against a dribbler and shooter?
- What are the most effective ways to score a goal?
- What are the most effective ways to prevent a goal from being scored?

Adapted, by permission, from J. Byl, 2004, *101 fun warm-up and cool-down games* (Champaign, IL: Human Kinetics), 148.

OFFENSIVE ATTACK

Objective

For the offensive team: to score on the defending team; for the defensive team: to get the ball away from the offensive team

Specific Skill Focus

Passing, dribbling, shooting, catching, guarding, and blocking (basketball, soccer, hockey)

Equipment

Hockey sticks, one ball, and one net (either a real net or an empty garbage can or plastic hoop)

Setup

- Mark off a playing area with lines 5 to 10 steps wide, or use a space such as a driveway.
- The offensive team begins at the end line (or sidewalk), and the defensive team begins in the playing area (or driveway).
- The net (or garbage can) is set on the far end or against the garage door.

How to Play

- Play begins when the offensive player passes the ball in to a teammate.
- Offensive teammates dribble, pass, and finally shoot on the net.
- Defensive players guard, block, and try to get the ball away from an offensive player without a foul (excessive body contact).
- If the offensive team scores, they get one point. The ball is then given to the other team to begin their offensive attack, beginning again from the end line or sidewalk.
- If, however, the defensive team manages to gain possession of the ball, they are awarded a point, play stops, and they line up at the end line or sidewalk for their offensive attack.

He shoots, he scores!

Variations

- Change the size and height of the net. Substitute a cone or outdoor chair, and count a hit as a point.
- Add a rule that a team can attempt to score only after making at least three passes.
- Add a rule that if the defensive team can get the ball out of bounds, by knocking it out of the hands of an offensive player, they can stop play and become the offensive team, although they won't score a point for this.

Questions for Understanding

- How does the game change when players call to each other (e.g., "Pass to me!" or "I'm open!" or "To you, Jim?")?
- Is it easier to defend a low-bounce dribble or a high-bounce dribble?
- Where is it most effective to place your arms when trying to block an offensive player?
- Where is the best place for your body when you are trying to cover another offensive player who is hoping to receive a pass?

ONE-GOAL SOCCER

Objective

To score more goals than the opponent does

Specific Skill Focus

Dribbling (soccer, hockey)

Equipment

One soccer ball and two cones per game

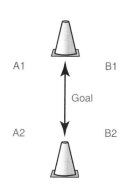

Setup

- Set up two cones two steps apart as a goal.
- Two players per team each stand on the opposite side of the same goal; one team has the ball.

How to Play

- One team of two players begins with the ball and attempts to dribble and pass by the opposing team and kick the ball into the goal.
- The other team tries to prevent a goal and also tries to intercept the ball and score.
- For the other team to score a goal, they must first pass or dribble the ball to the other side of the goal.
- After a team has scored a goal, the team scored against gets to dribble the ball three steps from the goal before the other team can defend against them.

Questions for Understanding

- What are the best ways to control the dribble so that the opponent does not get the ball?
- What are the best ways to get past the defense to score?
- What are the best ways to defend against a dribbler and shooter?

Adapted, by permission, from J. Byl, 2004, *101 fun warm-up and cool-down games* (Champaign, IL: Human Kinetics), 149.

TWO GOALKEEPERS

Objective
To try to score goals against two goalkeepers

Specific Skill Focus
Kicking (soccer)

Equipment
One ball and one goal (or markers to identify a goal)

Setup
- Have one goal with two goalies in it.
- Have one defensive player in front of the goalies.
- Have two strikers outside the penalty area. Five players is ideal for this game.

How to Play
- The leader rolls a ball to one of the strikers.
- The strikers dribble, pass, or shoot until they score or the ball goes past the goal.
- Repeat 10 times and count how many goals they score.

Variation
Increase the players to three strikers and two defenders.

Questions for Understanding
- How does a striker increase the success of his shooting?
- How do the defenders and goalies decrease the success of the strikers?

HIT IT DOWN OR INTERCEPT

Objective

To teach the defenders how to intercept a ball or hit it down; to teach proper positioning in order to get a good angle on the ball

Specific Skill Focus

Catching, dodging, jumping, overhand throwing, and running (disc, football)

Equipment

One football or one disc and two cones

Setup

Set up cones 20 steps apart. The defensive player stands between the two cones.

How to Play

- There will be a quarterback, a receiver, and a defender.
- The receiver will run a straight route from the first cone to the second cone while the defender keeps space between the offense and then tries to get an interception by either catching the ball or hitting it down.
- The quarterback will try to hit the receiver with a pass.
- After several plays, everyone rotates to the next position.

Variation

After doing straight routes, let the receivers run slants and cuts and mix up the route each time.

Questions for Understanding

- Why would you hit the ball down?
- What's the best way to intercept the ball?
- What's the best way for the offense to complete a pass?

MIRROR

Objective

To build shadowing skills to gain control of the ball

Specific Skill Focus

Dodging, dribbling, and running (soccer, basketball, disc, football, lacrosse, hockey)

Equipment

None

Setup

The defender stands in front of a partner, facing him a couple of steps away.

How to Play

When the whistle is blown, the offensive player starts to run down the field, while the defender keeps a couple of steps between himself and his partner while sidestepping in a backward direction, mirroring his movements.

Variation

When players are getting the hang of it and both partners have had a turn, the offensive player starts making cuts to the left and right while the defender tries to mirror the movements.

Questions for Understanding

- Why is keeping space important?
- What body movements help you know which direction change your offensive player is going to make?

SLIDERS

Objective

To see how far players can slide

Specific Skill Focus

Sliding (baseball, soccer)

Equipment

Measuring tape

Setup

- On a rainy day or when the dew is on the grass, have a player stand on the grass about five steps away from a starting line.
- Be sure the area is free from anything that might cut the player, such as rocks, glass, or other dangerous protruding objects.

How to Play

The player takes a run at the line and then slides feet first to see how far she can slide.

Questions for Understanding

- What makes sliding safer?
- What makes sliding more effective?

TAIL TAG

Objective

For the students to be quick on their feet and aware of their surroundings

Specific Skill Focus

Dodging, hopping, jumping, and running (football)

Equipment

A flag

Setup

- Two or three players stand in a straight line facing each other's backs. They must remain in contact at all times by placing their hands on the hips of the person in front.
- The player at the back of the line has a flag hanging out of the back of the top of his pants.
- A tagger stands facing the front player in the line.

The whole team tries to protect the tail in Tail Tag.

How to Play

- The goal of the game is for the tagger to get the flag.
- The two or three players move as a unit, trying to keep the tagger away from the player at the back.
- Once the tagger gets the flag, switch roles.

Variation

Play with two or more teams of two or three players, with each back player having a flag. Each team tries to get the other team's flag without losing their own.

Questions for Understanding

- What are things the line can do to keep them from losing their flag?
- What are things the tagger can do to help her grab the flag?

NET AND WALL GAMES

Work is not the opposite of play, depression is.
Dr. Stuart Brown

Racket sports and volleyball involve hitting a ball or shuttle over a net. These types of learning games form the basis of this chapter. Racket sports include tennis, badminton, Speedminton, and table tennis. Because rackets make striking an object more difficult, they are often introduced at simple levels for younger players, who learn more control as they get older. Many of the racket games in this section are introductory. You can also make things easier by using wooden tennis rackets (purchase them at yard sales) with half the handle cut off so the racket is shorter and by using sponge tennis balls rather than real tennis balls.

The prime objective of net and wall games is to propel a ball or shuttle or other object into the air in such a manner that the opponent cannot make a successful return. The only time a player holds the object in her hand is when she is putting the object into play with a serve. To play these games well, the player must have sound mechanics and must carefully consider and execute the attack—proper placement of the object is of central importance. Selecting the right shot, analyzing the location of the players on the court, and using body fakes are all important in winning a point. When defending against an attack, players need to cover the playing area well to defend their space and set up for as strong an attack as possible.

BALANCE RACE

Objective

To run to the net and back as many times as possible in 2 minutes while keeping an object on the racket

Specific Skill Focus

Racket familiarization (badminton, tennis)

Equipment

One racket and one ball (or shuttle) per player

Setup

A player stands on the baseline or end line of a tennis or badminton court holding a racket with a ball or shuttle resting on the racket. This drill can also be done on a driveway or grassy space.

How to Play

- On the signal to begin, the player runs as quickly as possible to the net and back without dropping the ball or shuttle.
- If the object drops, note the time and have the player begin again from the start to see if he can beat that time before the 2-minute time limit is up.

Variation

Younger players can place a beanbag on the racket to make this challenge easier.

Questions for Understanding

- What can you change to more easily keep your ball or shuttle on the racket?
- Where should you look when traveling in order to keep your ball or shuttle in place?

DROP BALL

Objective
To get as many consecutive hits as possible

Specific Skill Focus
Striking and throwing (badminton, tennis, baseball)

Equipment
One racket or paddle per player and a number of balls (or shuttles)

Setup
- The player stands perpendicular to the intended target.
- The tosser stands directly in front of the player.

How to Play
- The tosser tosses the ball (or shuttle) so that it bounces or moves right in front of the stroke area (backhand or forehand).
- The player executes a correct stroke or hit.
- Count how many consecutive strokes the player can make.

Questions for Understanding
- How can you increase the likelihood of successfully hitting the ball?
- Is it easier to complete the stroke with knees straight or bent?

NO-NET CONSECUTIVE HITS

Objective
To get as many consecutive hits as possible

Specific Skill Focus
Striking and throwing (badminton, tennis, baseball)

Equipment
One racket or bat and one ball per player

Setup
The player stands approximately five steps from the tosser—no net is used. The tosser is positioned with her back to a large fence or wall to make retrieving the ball easier.

How to Play
- The tosser bounces or tosses the ball to the desired spot (forehand, or backhand, or a mixture) in front of the hitter.
- The hitter uses the correct stroke or swing to hit or bunt the ball back to the tosser.
- Count how many correct and consecutive hits the hitter can accomplish.

Variations
- Consecutive Hits With a Net: Count the consecutive hits made over a tennis net (tosser throws the ball from the opposite side of the net).
- Long Hits: The player begins at the back of the service box. If she is successful in hitting the ball over the net, she takes a step backward; if she is unsuccessful in hitting the ball over the net, she takes a step forward. Play again.

Questions for Understanding
- How can you change your ready position to improve your hits?
- How does standing sideways to the thrower change your ability to hit the ball or shuttle?

WALL BALL

Objective

To get as many consecutive hits as possible

Specific Skill Focus

Striking and throwing (badminton, tennis)

Equipment

One racket and one ball per player

Setup

A player stands perpendicular to a wall, about 5 to 10 steps away, holding a racket and a ball.

How to Play

A player hits the ball against a wall and counts how many consecutive hits he can make.

Variations

- Distance Wall Ball: Add a line the player must stand behind when hitting the ball. Increase the distance from the wall as the player's skills improve.
- Partners Wall Ball: Alternate hits with two or more players.

Questions for Understanding

- How can you control the ball in the best way?
- How can you plan where to stand in order to best return the ball or shuttle?

BEANBAG TOSS TO PARTNER

Objective
To successfully serve a beanbag to a partner the most consecutive times

Specific Skill Focus
Service (volleyball)

Equipment
One beanbag or ball per pair of players

Setup
Two players stand opposite each other approximately four steps apart. One player holds a beanbag.

How to Play
- The player with the beanbag does an underhand throw to his partner.
- The partner catches the beanbag and then does an underhand throw back to his partner.
- Players count the number of successful consecutive passes in which a throw is made and caught without the catcher needing to move too far away to catch the beanbag.

Variations
- Each time a successful toss and catch are made, both players take one step back. When a pass or catch is unsuccessful, both players take one step forward. Players try to see how far away from each other they can get and still catch each other's throws.
- Serve a Ball to Partner: The players serve a volleyball underhand to a partner. Begin with players standing close by, and then add distance and a net to serve the ball over.

Questions for Understanding
- How can you make the ball or beanbag easier or more difficult to catch for your partner?
- When you are catching, how do you estimate where your hands should be to receive the toss?

FOREARM FOUR SQUARE

Objective

To advance to the king's or queen's court by successfully using a forearm pass into each other's squares

Specific Skill Focus

Forearm pass (volleyball)

Equipment

One volleyball

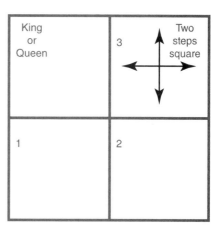

Setup

- Draw a four-square box as shown in the figure, with each section approximately two steps square.
- Players stand in each of the squares; the player in the king or queen square holds the ball and begins play.

How to Play

- The queen (or king) tosses the ball up and does a forearm pass that goes higher than her waist and bounces on the ground inside one of her opponent's squares.
- The player in whose square the ball lands must forearm pass the ball so that it goes higher than her waist and lands inside one of her opponent's squares.
- If a player does not hit the ball high enough, or does not hit the ball inside one of her opponent's squares, she is out.
- When a player is out, she goes to the number 1 square and everyone else moves up one square (in other words, if the player in number 2 makes an error, player 2 goes to the number 1 square and the player in the number 1 square goes to number 2; if the player in number 3 makes an error, then this player goes to the number 1 square, the player in the number 1 square goes to number 2, and the player

in the number 2 square goes to number 3; if the king or queen is dethroned by making a mistake, that player goes to the number 1 square, the other players move up one square, and the player that was in number 3 becomes the new king or queen).

- The king or queen gets the ball and begins play again.

Variation

Four square can also be played with two or three players, with the court outlined as shown in the figures.

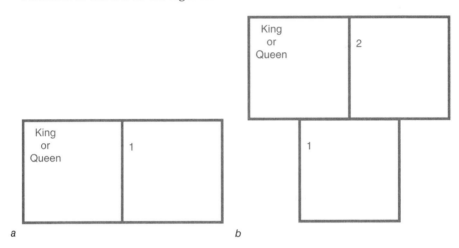

a   *b*

Questions for Understanding

- How can you most effectively get other players out?
- How can you control the direction of the ball with a forearm pass?

MINI VOLLEYBALL

Objective

To count how many consecutive times players can toss a ball over a net, have the opposing player hit it, and then have the first player catch it.

Specific Skill Focus

Throwing, hitting, and catching (volleyball)

Equipment

A net or rope hung about one and a half steps high and one beach ball per pair of players

Setup

A player stands on either side of the net, and one player holds a ball. Make a court with ropes or other markers that is approximately four steps wide and four steps deep on either side of the net.

How to Play

- The player with the beach ball underhand serves the ball over the net to the player on the opposite side.
- The player who receives the ball hits the ball back over the net to the player on the other side, who catches it. This player then tosses it again. Each successful hit over the net scores one point. Players try to cooperatively get the most points. Change roles after ten points.

Variation

Players can begin with a beach ball and then go to a regular volleyball if they are skilled enough.

Questions for Understanding

- To improve the receiving player's chances of hitting the ball, where should you throw the ball, and how do you make sure the other player knows where the ball is going?
- When hitting the tossed ball, where should you hit the ball to improve the tosser's chances of catching it?

NET TOSS

Objective

To count how many consecutive times players can toss a ball over a net, successfully catch it, and toss it back again

Specific Skill Focus

Throwing and catching (volleyball)

Equipment

A net or rope hung about one and a half steps high and one volleyball per pair of players

Setup

A player stands on either side of the net, and one player holds a ball.

How to Play

- The player with the ball tosses the ball over the net to the player on the opposite side. If the player catches the ball, a point is scored.
- The player who caught the ball now tosses the ball back over the net; if the ball is caught, another point is scored.
- Players keep tossing the ball back and forth and count how many consecutive passes they can make until the toss does not go over the net or the ball is not caught.
- Players can play cooperatively, working together for highest score, or competitively, making it more challenging for their opponent to catch the ball.

Variation

Single Wall Toss: A player tosses a ball against a wall and then catches it after the wall bounce.

Questions for Understanding

- When playing cooperatively, where should you throw the ball, and how do you make sure the other player knows where the ball is going?
- When playing competitively, where should you throw the ball, and how do you fool the opposing player?

PARTNER NET TOSS

Objective

To count how many consecutive times players can toss a ball over a net, successfully catch it, and toss it back again

Specific Skill Focus

Throwing and catching (volleyball)

Equipment

A net or rope hung about one and a half steps high and one volleyball

Setup

Two players stand on either side of the net, and one player holds a ball.

How to Play

- The player with the ball tosses it over the net to the player on the opposite side. If the player catches the ball, a point is scored.
- The player who caught the ball tosses it to the teammate on her side of the net, who then tosses the ball back over the net; if it is caught, another point is scored.
- Players keep tossing the ball back and forth and count how many consecutive passes they can make until the toss does not go over the net or the ball is not caught.

Variations

- This game can also be played competitively, with players on each side trying to throw the ball over the net to a place where the other team is not. Boundaries will need to be established (perhaps a four-step square on either side of the net).
- Balloon Net Whack: Count how many times players can hit a balloon over the net. Played with partners, a player cannot hit the balloon twice in a row. Played cooperatively, count how many successful times the balloon can be hit across the net. To play competitively, each side scores a point if the other team fails to return the balloon before it hits the floor, if the balloon does not go over the net, or if it is hit outside the boundary lines.
- Beach Ball Net Whack: Played like Balloon Net Whack but with a beach ball.

Questions for Understanding

- When playing cooperatively, where should you throw the ball, and how do you make sure the other player knows where the ball is going?
- When playing competitively, where should you throw the ball, and how do you fool the opposing players?

PARTNER WALL SPIKE

Objective

To successfully spike the ball off a wall

Specific Skill Focus

Spiking (volleyball)

Equipment

One volleyball per pair of players

Setup

Put tape on a wall about two steps apart. It does not really matter how high the ball goes or how far it rebounds. Four steps marks the spot to serve from (closer to the wall if too difficult, and farther if too easy). A player holds a volleyball, ready to serve.

How to Play

- A player tosses the ball into the air and spikes it in front of the wall so it bounces up against the wall between the two pieces of tape and back to the player, who spikes the ball without catching it.
- Teammates keep the ball in play by alternately spiking the ball.
- Count how many consecutive times this can be done.

Variation

This game can also be played competitively; players gain a point and first service each time the partner fails to return their spike with a legal spike (against the floor and wall).

Questions for Understanding

- What makes it easiest to return the ball accurately?
- When playing competitively, what makes it difficult for the partner to return the ball?

WALL SPIKE

Objective
To successfully spike the ball off a wall

Specific Skill Focus
Spiking (volleyball)

Equipment
One volleyball per person

Setup
A player holds a volleyball and stands about four steps from a large flat wall.

How to Play
- The player tosses the ball into the air and spikes it in front of the wall so it bounces up against the wall and back to the player, who catches it.
- Count how many consecutive times this can be done.

Variation
Continuous Wall Spike: When the ball returns off the wall, the player spikes the ball again (either in the air or off one bounce from the ground—players do not catch the ball in this variation). Count how many consecutive spikes can be made.

Questions for Understanding
- How can you vary the targeted wall height to change the ball's return height?
- How does changing the bend at the elbow change the power as you hit the ball?

STRIKING AND FIELDING GAMES

Baseball is 90% mental—the other half is physical.

Yogi Berra

Striking a ball with a bat is challenging because the ball is moving at different speeds and trajectories. Fielding a ball hit off a bat is also challenging because the ball is often coming at the player with considerable speed and perhaps bouncing somewhat wildly. This chapter contains games that teach striking and throwing, passing, fielding, and running bases.

The essence of striking and fielding games is that players strike an object. Points are scored if the object is hit out of the playing area or a run is scored. The game requires a striker or batter who, if the object is successfully hit, becomes a runner, as well as fielders who try to catch the object or get a runner out. Striking and fielding games are typically slower and tactically less complex, allowing more time for fewer decisions.

BASEBALL WITHOUT BASERUNNING

Objective

To score as many runs as possible

Specific Skill Focus

Catching, running, striking, and throwing (baseball)

Equipment

One bat, one ball, three cones, and two baseball gloves

Setup

- Place the two cones about 5 steps apart and about 10 steps from home plate (third cone).
- One player is at bat at home plate, another player is in front of the two cones, and a third player is behind the two cones.
- If you have four players, have two teams of two, with players taking turns batting when their team is up.

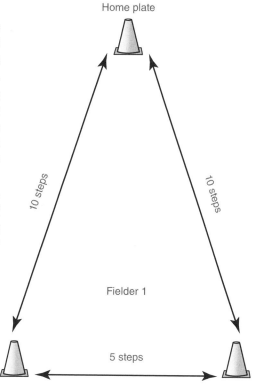

Home plate

10 steps

10 steps

Fielder 1

5 steps

Fielder 2

How to Play

- The batter tosses the ball to himself and hits the ball. If the ball
  - rolls past the first fielder and is stopped by the second fielder, it is a single;
  - lands past the first fielder and is stopped by the second fielder, it is a double;
  - rolls past the second fielder, it is a triple; or
  - goes over the head of the second fielder, it is a home run.
- Imaginary players on base can move forward only one base ahead of where the hitter ends up.
  - No one runs any bases, but the player positions are shouted out after each successful hit.
  - For example, if a hitter hits a double, there is a player on second. If a player then hits another double, there is a player on second and third. If a player then hits a single, there is a player on first, second, and third. If a player then hits a double, there is a player on second and third, and two runs score.
- It is a strike if a batter misses the ball, if a batter hits a foul ball (outside the cones), or if the fielder standing in front of the cones catches the rolling ball.
- A batter is out if he gets three strikes in a row or if a hit is caught in the air before hitting the ground.
- When there are three outs, the batter becomes the near fielder, the near fielder goes back to the deep outfield, and the deep outfielder comes up to bat.
- If you are playing with two teams of two players, then the players can decide between them who plays in front of the cones and who plays behind the cones.

Questions for Understanding

- How does moving the cones closer together or farther apart or closer to home plate or farther from home plate affect the level of difficulty of the game?
- When batting, can you change the way you are standing to influence where the ball goes?

GHOST BASEBALL

Objective
To score the highest number of runs for your team

Specific Skill Focus
Catching, running, striking, and throwing (baseball)

Equipment
Bases, gloves, bat, and ball

Setup
- Set up two teams, with three players per team.
- One team goes out to the field; the other team lines up at the bench, and one player prepares to bat.
- The pitcher can be an adult instructor.
- This game allows a small number of participants to make two teams and still play a regular game of baseball.

How to Play
- The first player from the hitting team hits the ball and makes it to a base.
- The second player is a "ghost player," and this imaginary player automatically gets a one-base hit, forcing the first player to second base.
- The next player goes to bat and, if successful, makes it to first or second base, pushing the ghost player to second and the first player to third, or the ghost to third and the runner home.
- Two real players must leave a base between them for the ghost player.
- Play continues, with every other batter as a ghost player.
- Only runs scored by the real players count as team runs.

Questions for Understanding
- Where can you hit the ball to gain the most time on your run?
- How can the defensive team determine where the most important out will be on the field?

NOODLE PADDLE

Objective

To hit a balloon a set distance as quickly as possible

Specific Skill Focus

Running and striking (baseball)

Equipment

One pool noodle (cut in half), one balloon, and a watch with a second hand

Setup

- One player stands behind a start line and holds a balloon in one hand and a pool noodle in the other.
- Establish a finish line 20 steps away.

How to Play

On the signal to start, the player hits the balloon in the air with the pool noodle, striking it hard and repeatedly in an effort to get the balloon from the start line to the finish line in as little time as possible.

Variation

Count how few hits a player can use to get the balloon to the finish line.

Questions for Understanding

- How can you most effectively strike the balloon so it goes the farthest each time?
- Is it more effective to wait for the balloon to settle or to keep it in constant motion with the noodle?

RECORD FOR DISTANCE

Objective

To throw a disc (or ball) as far as possible from behind a line

Specific Skill Focus

Overhand throwing and throwing (basketball, disc, football, lacrosse, baseball)

Equipment

A plastic disc (or a ball) and a long measuring device

Setup

Place a starting line at one end of a long open field.

How to Play

- The player throws the disc or ball as far as possible.
- Measure the length of the throw by counting the steps or using a measuring device from the starting line to where the disc or ball lands.

Variation

Distance in Time: The player throws the disc as far as possible and follows it. Once the disc lands, the player picks it up and throws it again and follows it. Measure how far the player is after 1 minute (or another preset time).

Questions for Understanding

- What are the key elements of throwing for distance?
- When do you release your breath during the throw?

For world records, go to www.wfdf.org/history-stats/world-records. For 12 more disc games, go to www.teammakers.com/overview.aspx.

RECORD FOR MAXIMUM TIME ALOFT

Objective

To toss the disc (or ball) and catch it, trying for the longest time in between throwing and catching

Specific Skill Focus

Overhand throwing and throwing (basketball, disc, football, lacrosse, baseball)

Equipment

A plastic disc and a timing device

Setup

A player stands in the middle of a large field with the disc.

How to Play

- A player tosses the disc high into the sky. As soon as the disc leaves the thrower's hand, begin the timer.
- The player must then catch the disc (if it is not caught, then the throw does not count). As soon as the player catches the disc, stop the timer.

Questions for Understanding

- How can you increase the time aloft and still catch the disc?
- How can you estimate wind direction and change your throw to let the wind help your time?

For world records, go to www.wfdf.org/history-stats/world-records.

SOCCER BASEBALL

Objective

To score more runs than an opponent by kicking a ball far and then dribbling a ball around the bases

Specific Skill Focus

Catching, dribbling, kicking, and running (soccer, baseball)

Equipment

Two soccer balls and three cones

Setup

- Place the two cones (first and second bases) about 5 steps apart and about 10 steps from home plate.
- Place two soccer balls at home base.
- One kicker stands at home, and the other two players stand in the field—one in the infield (before the cones) and the other in the outfield (behind the cones).

How to Play

- The kicker kicks the ball off the ground and then runs around the two bases and back home. If the kicker is successful, she earns one run, waits for everyone to get set, and goes again.
- The two fielders trap the ball (no use of hands) and kick the ball to arrive at home base before the kicker returns. If the outfielders are successful, the kicker is out. When the kicker is out she goes into the outfield, the outfielder comes into the infield, and the infielder becomes the new kicker.

Variation

Soccer Baseball With Dribble: Have two balls at the home base. The kicker kicks one ball into the outfield and then dribbles the second ball around the bases.

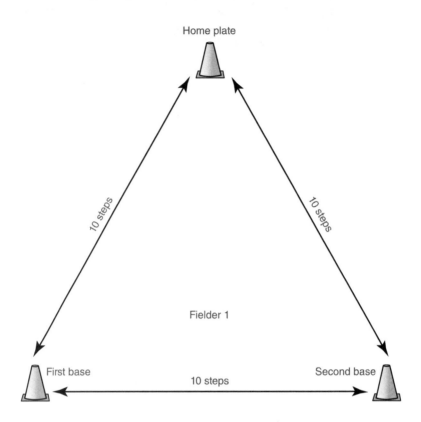

Home plate

10 steps

10 steps

Fielder 1

First base

10 steps

Second base

Fielder 2

Questions for Understanding

- How does reducing or increasing the space between the cones make the game easier or more difficult?
- How can you change your body position before the kick to control where the ball will go?

TEEING OFF

Objective

To hit as many balls as possible from different locations

Specific Skill Focus

Striking (baseball)

Equipment

A baseball tee and five baseballs

Setup

Set up a baseball tee at home plate; place one baseball on the tee and put the others nearby.

How to Play

- The batter sees how many balls she can hit a good distance—the batter should imagine the pitch leaving a pitcher's hands.
- The batter stays in the same stance for five hits, and then the tee is adjusted for the next five hits. The different stances are as follows:
  - In the middle of the plate
  - High on the inside of the plate
  - Low on the outside of the plate
  - High on the outside of the plate
  - Low on the inside of the plate
- After hitting five balls, the batter retrieves the balls while the instructor adjusts the tee.

Questions for Understanding

- What important changes do you need to make to adjust to different pitching locations?
- How can you change body positions to make the swing more accurate?

THROW FOR POINTS

Objective

To earn points by throwing to places where it is difficult to make a catch and then to successfully catch those throws

Specific Skill Focus

Catching and throwing (baseball, basketball, football, disc, lacrosse)

Equipment

One baseball glove per player, one ball per pair of players, and a timing device

Setup

The players stand 10 steps apart, and one player holds the ball.

Catching for points.

How to Play

- The players have 2 minutes to score as many points as possible by throwing a ball back and forth to each other.
- Scoring is as follows:
  - No points for a ball that bounces twice before it is caught or a ball that is dropped.
  - One point for a throw caught below the waist.
  - Two points for a throw caught above the shoulders.
  - Three points for a throw caught below the shoulders and above the waist.
  - Four points for a throw caught off one bounce.

Variation

To increase the difficulty for better throwers, have the two players move farther apart.

Questions for Understanding

- What are the key considerations for getting the most points and not wasting throws by getting zero points?
- When catching, where should your gaze be in order to catch the most balls?

PASSING VOLLEYBALLS

Objective

To make as many consecutive passes as possible

Specific Skill Focus

Setting and forearm passing (volleyball)

Equipment

One volleyball per player

Setup

The player stands in an open area holding a volleyball.

How to Play

The player tosses the ball up and begins to set (or forearm pass) the ball to herself and counts how many consecutive passes she can make.

Variations

- Partner Passing: Players pair up and face each other about three or four steps apart. The player with the ball tosses the ball to his partner, who then sets (or forearm passes) the ball back to his partner, who catches it. The players count how many consecutive correct passes they can make.
- Partner Continuous Passing: Players pair up and face each other about three or four steps apart. The player with the ball tosses the ball to his partner, who then sets (or forearm passes) the ball back to his partner, who then sets (or forearm passes) the ball back. The players count how many consecutive passes they can make.
- Wall Passing: A player tosses the ball up and begins to set (or forearm pass) the ball against a wall, counting how many consecutive passes she can make.
- Triangle (or Square) Passing: Have three or four players passing one ball to each other and counting how many consecutive passes they can make (try it with two balls for extra craziness and requiring extra communication on the part of the players).

Questions for Understanding

- What are the keys to making these passes successful in terms of positioning of the body, the way the hands contact the ball, and the height of the pass (square to the direction of the intended receiver)?
- Does greater ball height make it easier or harder to return the pass?

QUICK RELAY PASS

Objective
To complete as many relay passes as possible in 1 minute

Specific Skill Focus
Catching, kicking, overhand throwing, and throwing (soccer, basketball, disc, football, lacrosse, hockey, baseball)

Equipment
One ball, a glove for each player, and a timing device

Setup
Three players stand in a line, approximately 15 steps away from the player in the middle. The player at one end holds the ball.

Quick Relay Pass.

How to Play

- On the signal to begin, the player at the end throws the ball to the middle player, who catches it, turns, and passes it to the player at the other end of the line. The player at the other end of the line catches the ball and passes it back to the middle player, who catches it, turns, and passes it back to the first player.
- Count how many times the middle player catches the ball in 1 minute.
- Have players switch positions so that each player has an opportunity to do the relay pass in the middle.

Player 1   Player 2   Player 3

15 steps   15 steps

Questions for Understanding

- What are keys for the middle player to remember when executing quick relay passes?
- How does your foot position affect your throw or pass when you turn?

RESTING VOLLEY

Objective

To make as many consecutive volleys as possible

Specific Skill Focus

Volleying (volleyball)

Equipment

One balloon or volleyball per player

Setup

The player lies on his back, holding a balloon or volleyball.

How to Play

- While lying on his back, the player counts how many consecutive volleys he can make using the finger pads of both hands.
- Begin with a balloon because it is easier than using a real volleyball. Advance to a real volleyball when players are ready.

Variation

- Two-Player Resting Volley: Two players lie opposite each other, with their heads close together and feet farthest apart. Players pass the balloon or ball back and forth to each other and count how many consecutive passes they can complete.
- Weighted Balloon: Add a layer of duct tape or masking tape over the balloon's surface to give it some weight.

Questions for Understanding

- What part of the hand makes for the most accurate passes?
- Where should the elbows be to make this challenge easier?
- How does increasing the spread of your fingers affect your control of the balloon?

CATCH WHAT YOU CAN

Objective

To catch as many balls as possible in 1 minute

Specific Skill Focus

Catching (lacrosse)

Equipment

One lacrosse stick per pair of players and 10 or more balls

Setup

- The player with the stick stands three or four steps away from his partner.
- The partner piles the balls at his feet.

How to Play

- When the timer starts, the player tosses the balls by hand to the catcher, aiming for the pocket.
- The catcher attempts to catch each ball and gently passes the ball back to the thrower.

Accurately timed catches.

- The team counts how many successful catches they make in 1 minute.

Variations

- Between catches, the catcher shuffles back and forth between two cones. The thrower can also shuffle back and forth between two cones between throws. For older players, use one ball and have the pair move up and down a field during this drill.
- Two Ball: Each player has a ball, and the pairs toss and catch simultaneously.

Questions for Understanding

- How can the thrower change the speed of the throw to make it easier for the catcher to get the ball in the pocket?
- What stick position is best for catching?
- How does the distance between partners affect success?

FIVE HUNDRED

Objective

To catch or retrieve a ball and score 500 points or more

Specific Skill Focus

Catching, overhand throwing, running, striking, and throwing (disc, football, lacrosse, baseball)

Equipment

One ball and one bat per game and one baseball glove per fielder

Setup

On a large field, position a batter at one end and one or several receivers in the outfield.

How to Play

- The batter tosses the ball to herself and hits it toward the outfielders.
- The outfielders try to catch the ball.
- If an outfielder catches the ball, then her catch is scored as follows:
  - 25 points for catching a rolling ball
  - 50 points for catching a ball that bounced twice
  - 75 points for catching a ball that bounced only once
  - 100 points for catching a fly ball
- If the infielder drops the ball on one of these plays, the points are subtracted from the score.
- Once an outfielder reaches 500 points, she becomes the new batter.

Questions for Understanding

- When several outfielders are trying to catch the ball, how does a fielder stay focused on the ball?
- How can you guess where a bounced ball is going to go?

FREESTYLE DISCS

Objective
To explore different ways to catch, spin, and do other tricks with the disc

Specific Skill Focus
Catching, kicking, and throwing (soccer, basketball, disc, football)

Equipment
One disc per player or pair of players

Setup
A player or a pair of players stand in an open area with one disc.

How to Play
Players explore how many different ways they can catch, spin, or do other tricks with the disc. For example, players might toss the disc up behind their backs and catch it in front of their bodies, or toss it up from under one leg and catch it with the same hand underneath the other leg.

Questions for Understanding
- How can you change your grip on the disc to control its movements?
- How can you use the wind to affect your disc's flight?

For some great ideas for challenges you can do inside, do an Internet search for "Frisbee freestyle video."

LONG TRAP

Objective

To effectively kick, throw, volley or trap a ball from farther distances

Specific Skill Focus

Kicking, throwing, volleying, and trapping (soccer)

Equipment

One ball for each pair of players

Setup

Two players stand five steps apart, and one holds a ball.

How to Play

- For trapping:
  - The player with the ball rolls the ball to the other player.
  - The receiving player traps the ball with the sole of his foot.
- If successful, then both players take a step back. The receiving player rolls the ball to the other player, who now receives it.
- If players are unsuccessful, they take a step forward.
- See how far apart players can get and remain successful.
- For kicking, throwing, volleying, or volleyball serving, use the same game but emphasize proper kicking, throwing, volleying, or volleyball serving technique.

Variations

- Instead of rolling the ball, the players bounce the ball to their partners.
- Specify the type of trap, kick, throw, or serve you want made.

Questions for Understanding

- What is the most effective way to trap a ball?
- What are important changes to improve accuracy and distance?

RECORD FOR THROW, RUN, AND CATCH

Objective

To see how far a player can throw a disc and still catch it

Specific Skill Focus

Catching, kicking, overhand throwing, running, and throwing (soccer, basketball, disc, football, lacrosse, baseball)

Equipment

A plastic disc and a measuring device

Setup

Place a starting line at one end of a long open field.

How to Play

- The player throws the disc as far as possible, chases after it, and catches it.
- If the disc is not caught, then the throw is invalid.
- Measure the distance from the throw to the catch.

Variation

Instead of a disc, try kicking a soccer ball or football, or throwing a basketball, football, lacrosse ball, or baseball.
For world records, go to www.wfdf.org/history-stats/world-records.

Questions for Understanding

- How can you maximize the distance thrown and still be able to catch the disc?
- How can the wind direction help or hinder your result?

ROLLERS

Objective

To catch hard-rolling balls and quickly toss the ball to first

Specific Skill Focus

Catching and throwing (baseball)

Equipment

Four bases, one ball, two gloves for groups of three players, and a timer

Setup

One player stands in shortstop position between second base and third base, and the other stands on first base while the instructor stands at home.

How to Play

- The instructor rolls grounders to the shortstop.
- The shortstop throws the ball to first, and the first-base player throws the ball home.
- Count how many consecutive passes the players make in 2 minutes, and then rotate the shortstop and first-base players.

Variation

The instructor hits grounders to the shortshop.

Questions for Understanding

- How can the players best position themselves to catch the rolling ball?
- How can you avoid a head hit when the ball bounces?

ROLLING GOALS

Objective

To prevent a player who is rolling balls toward a goal from scoring

Specific Skill Focus

Catching, rolling, kicking, goalkeeping (soccer)

Equipment

One ball and a goal (or two items to mark a goal)

Setup

- Make a goal 8 steps wide. One of the players stands in the goal.
- Mark a line 10 to 20 steps away. The other player stands there holding a ball in his hands.

How to Play

- One player has 10 shots to roll a ball past the goalie. Each shot that is stopped scores one point for the goalkeeper, and each shot that goes in the goal scores one point for the shooter.
- Switch roles and repeat a number of times.
- The player with the most points wins.

Variation

Bouncing Goals: The ball must bounce once before the goal line.

Questions for Understanding

- What are the best ways to score a goal?
- What are the best ways to stop a goal?

STEPPER-BOARD CATCH

Objective
To catch a stuffed animal in as many different ways as possible

Specific Skill Focus
Catching and jumping (football, baseball)

Equipment
One stepper board and one stuffed animal per player

Setup
- Place a small piece (one foot in length or more) of 2 × 4 board on the floor, with the wide part on the floor.
- Place a half-step-length of 1 × 4 board crossways on top of the 2 × 4 (with the small piece of 2 × 4 acting as a fulcrum); put the stuffed animal on the far end of the 1 × 4 board.

How to Play
- The player stomps on the 1 × 4, which flips the stuffed animal into the air.
- The player catches the stuffed animal.
- Count how many different ways the animal can be caught: one hand, two hands, one hand with one clap before catching the animal, one hand with two claps, by one of the feet, and so on.

Catching items launched from a stepper board.

Questions for Understanding

- What is the best way to get the animal high into the air and still make it easy to catch?
- How does the animal's flight change when you place it at different distances from the end of the 1 × 4?
- How does the animal's flight change when you place the 1 × 4 over the 2 × 4 at different places?

HOT BOX

Objective

To escape the hot box

Specific Skill Focus

Catching, running, and throwing (baseball)

Equipment

Two bases, one ball, and two gloves

Setup

- Position two bases 10 steps apart. Standing on each of the bases is a player wearing a baseball glove; one of those players holds a ball.
- The remaining player stands in between the two bases.

How to Play

- The player in the middle tries to safely touch one of the bases without getting tagged by a player holding a ball.
- Players holding the ball can move closer to the player in the middle and can pass the ball to each other.

Tagging a runner caught in the "hot box."

Questions for Understanding

- How can the player in the middle increase the likelihood of mistakes by the throwing players?
- How can the throwing players increase the likelihood they will tag the player in the middle?

Adapted, by permission, from J. Byl, 2004, *101 fun warm-up and cool-down games* (Champaign, IL: Human Kinetics), 103.

NO-DEFENSE RUNNING

Objective
To learn when to run from the bases

Specific Skill Focus
Running (baseball)

Equipment
Four bases, five baseballs, and one bat

Setup
At a baseball diamond, have one runner at first, one on second, and a batter (instructor) at home plate.

How to Play
- Depending on where the ball is hit, the runners run, wait, or wait and run. On a
  - ground ball, both runners run to the next base;
  - hard ground ball, both runners run two bases;
  - fly ball to right or center field, both runners wait, and then the runner on second runs to third after the ball is caught while the runner on first does not run; and
  - fly ball to left field, both runners wait.
- The instructor may add additional comments such as, "The fly ball is landing short of the fielder. Run!"
- After each run, the runners go back to first and second.

Questions for Understanding
- What are the keys for knowing when to run and when not to run?
- At what point can you predict where the ball will go?

DANCE

Every day brings a chance for you to draw in a breath,
kick off your shoes, and dance.

Oprah Winfrey

Put on some music with a good beat, and young and old begin to sway and move to the music. We were made to move to the beat. Any time we let ourselves go, we undoubtedly feel the gentle fatigue from active movement, the delight in "doing it right," and the joy in doing it at all. Dance is a part of the knowledge of physical education, and moving to music is an important part of physical literacy. Teaching physical education without dance is like teaching math without subtraction, or grammar without verbs. Let's begin with some simple instructions to make teaching a dance unit fun. Then you'll find suggestions for creating your own dances and a few samples of some more formalized dances. Enjoy moving to music!

DANCE INSTRUCTIONS: NO FEAR!

If you have fears about doing this unit, I can tell you I did as well at one point. I had fears going into dancing, or moving to music as we called it—fear of not getting the dance perfectly right each time. By perfectly right that meant doing it exactly as the whole world does it. What I failed to realize is that the whole world does not often do a dance the same way because dances are interpreted differently by different people. That realization gave me the freedom to interpret a piece of music differently. What I also failed to realize is that dancing is not primarily about perfectly replicating a preestablished routine but about living actively and moving to the beat of the music. When straying from our preestablished routine, quickly getting back on track is part of the fun of dancing.

DANCE INSTRUCTIONS MADE EASY AND FUN

The key to dance is to keep it fun, simple, and balanced. In terms of the music and routines, make choices that keep the activity fun to do. Dances often begin with great music, and you can involve the children when making selections. Choose music with a strong 4/4 beat, and have students do each move for 8 beats. The selected song can be a popular song, a fun dance tune with some fiddle music, or even a worship song in which the lyrics are choreographed.

An overly complex routine will be frustrating for the participants, and an overly simple routine will be boring. Try to use and develop routines that challenge the dancers. As your students become more proficient, add scarves or balls to the routines for added challenge, beauty, and joy. Keep the dances physically balanced. In other words, when using a movement that takes you forward, then also add something that moves you backward; if you kick or punch or do another movement to the right, also do a kick or punch or other movement to the left.

Some musicians play by heart, but most do not. Most need sheet music in front of them. We do not need to know our dances by heart either—especially when we are just learning them. Writing key points on bristol board or a large piece of paper is an easy way to help dancers remember the sequence of steps. For the dancers and for you, as an instructor, having the key dance moves outlined clearly will help you keep track of the dance as you lead or engage in it.

The dances in this chapter can all be done in very small steps in more confined spaces and are great for daily physical activity breaks during your school day. Like the other activities, try to plan for a culminating activity at some future date. Have the dancers publicly perform the dances at small gatherings, such as in front of their own families, or slightly larger meetings, such as a homeschool meeting of several families, or a larger function like a worship service.

OVERALL MOVEMENT PATTERNS

Dances are built through four major elements, each with various contrasting movement patterns as shown in table 7.1. Time is an essential element of music, which can have a fast beat or a slow one (or differing

Table 7.1 Overall Movement Patterns

Element	Contrasting movements
Time	Fast/slow Increasing/decreasing On beat/off beat Short/long
Space	Large/small One spot/through space Straight/crooked Wide/narrow
Force	Explosive/gentle Heavy/light Moving/stopping Sharp/smooth Strong/soft Tight/loose
Shape	Right/left Forward/backward High/low Big/little Out/in

speeds throughout the music). Music is usually danced to on the beat, but sometimes it is interesting to dance part of the movements on the off beats, and the music can be a short piece or a longer one.

We dance in a space. Our movements in this large or small space can be in one spot or throughout that space. We can move in straight or crooked lines, using wide or narrow lanes. Our movements can include combinations of different intensities of force and can be explosive, heavy, moving, sharp, strong, tight, or their opposites: gentle, light, stopping, smooth, soft, or loose. We shape our dances through moving our bodies to the right and left, moving forward and backward, moving high and low, making ourselves big and little, moving out from a starting spot and back in. As you begin to create dances, encourage the dancers to build these different elements into their routines.

CREATING YOUR OWN DANCES

There are several ways to introduce dance. For younger children, help them choreograph songs they can sing to such as "Baa Baa Black Sheep," "Hickory Dickory Dock," or "Hokey Pokey." Most of these songs are readily available and can be downloaded off the Internet. This chapter presents four creative ideas. The first involves students following the leader. The second idea is creating a dance over an X pattern on the floor. Next, students learn to match certain dance moves to a music selection. Finally, students engage in free movement by exploring different movements to pieces of music. Let's do an example of each of these.

FOLLOW THE LEADER

Objective

To use various dance steps and follow a dance leader

Specific Skill Focus

Dance

Equipment

CD player and a suitable music CD

Setup

Students stand in a line, one behind the other.

How to Play

- When the music begins, have the first student in line lead the other students around the room with some kind of dance step for 16 beats.
- When the 16 beats are completed, the leader goes to the back of the line, and the new player in front of the line leads the others through 16 beats of music but to a different dance step.
- For dance step ideas, refer to Dance Cards for Line Dancing later in this chapter.
- Each student may wish to teach her dance step before adding the music.
- When the first leader comes to the front again, have her repeat the same dance movement, and continue this until the song is over. If the students are able, they could also lead two or more different dance moves, leading a different dance step each time they lead.
- Use different types of music and repeat.

Questions for Understanding

- What impact does different music have on the types of dances we do?
- How does increasing or decreasing your space change your steps?

X DANCE

Objective

To develop and demonstrate dances around an X

Specific Skill Focus

Dance

Equipment

CD player, a suitable music CD, and some tape to mark an X

Setup

Mark two Xs on the floor, and have each student stand with both feet straddling one line on their own X.

How to Play

- Have students develop and demonstrate an easily reproducible and repeatable eight-beat movement through the X.
- This movement could be as simple as hopping counterclockwise around the X by hopping on every other beat; or it could involve stepping forward with the right foot, forward with the left foot, backward with the right foot, backward with the left foot, and repeating this sequence—students could add arm movements as well to their steps, such as swinging the arms or punching one way and then the other.
- The steps could also be more complicated such as stepping forward with the left foot in front of the right foot, then the right foot crosses in front of the left into the front left space, then the left foot goes back to the original spot and the right foot goes back to the original spot. Then repeat with the right foot going in front of the left foot. The variations are numerous.
- After mastering several steps, the student can move through 8 beats of one step into 8 beats of another and then repeat the 16 beats or add a couple new steps before repeating 32 beats of music and dancing.

Variations

- Have the students teach others their dance.
- Use different music for the same routines.

Questions for Understanding

- What makes the dance exciting to do and watch but still simple enough to remember, replicate, and execute?
- When learning another student's dance, is it easier to have the leader face you or face away? Why?

DANCE CARDS FOR LINE DANCING

Objective

To develop and demonstrate new dances formed by using dance cards

Specific Skill Focus

Dance

Equipment

CD player and a suitable music CD

Setup

Prepare the dance cards.

How to Play

- Students use dance step cards to create their own dance (usually switching steps every 8 or 16 beats).
- On a different recipe card for each dance step, write out the following (and feel free to add your own dance steps):
    - Alternating knee lifts: Lift one knee, then the other. Option: As knee is raised, bring straight arms down on each side of raised knee.
    - Butterfly arms: Circle arms out and above head, hands crossed above head. Lower arms to front, crossing slightly at bottom.
    - Can-can: With your inside arms over each other's shoulders (or hands on waist), jump on both feet, lift right knee up while hopping on left; jump on both feet; kick right leg to left side while hopping on left; jump on both feet. Repeat with left leg.
    - Chicken jacks: Do jumping jacks, but tuck your hands under your armpits as if you are a chicken.
    - Digs: Pretend to dig with a shovel left to right while stepping onto right foot. Pivot on right foot then repeat to left. Optional: Add a clap as direction is changing.
    - Grapevine: Step out to right, cross left foot behind right, step out to right, then tap left foot beside right foot (or jump feet together). Repeat to left.
    - Hole in the fence: Step side to side. While stepping sideways, duck your head as if moving through a hole in a fence. Your

shoulders, arms, then rest of body follow your head as if moving through the hole. Repeat on the other side.

- Lasso: With arm out to side, bent at elbow with fist facing up, rotate your forearm and wrist as if swinging a lasso (two or four counts). Repeat on other side.
- Pogo jump: With arms tight to your sides, jump up and down, keeping body as straight and aligned as possible.
- Point to the foot: Dig your right heel diagonally out to the right while pointing your finger at the foot. Bring your foot back, and repeat on the left. Look at your foot while pointing at it.
- Polka step: Hop with quick steps right, left, right and then left, right, left. Continue.
- Raise the roof: With palms facing toward the roof, push arms up two times to the left, two times to the right.
- Sprinkler: Put one arm out front and bend other arm at the elbow, placing your hand behind your neck, elbow pointing to the side. Jerk the bent arm toward the straight arm as if you are watering the lawn with a sprinkler for four counts. Return elbow to start for four counts.
- Squish the bug: Bend right knee up, step out to right on ball of foot. Exaggerate push and twist into the ground three times. Repeat on left.
- V jump: Begin with feet together. Jump forward to a wide squat, bringing hands up to a "stop" action. Jump back, feet together, clapping two times.

- Give each student four cards.
- Have the students put together a dance with the dance steps outlined on the cards, repeating the four-step routine until the music ends.

Selected text reprinted, by permission, from CIRA Ontario, 2010, Move it to the beat – actions for music. In *Everybody move!: A multimedia package for daily physical activity*, 2nd ed. (Champaign, IL: Human Kinetics), 122-130.

Variations

- Use different music for the same routines.
- Have students write up their own dance steps on cards.

Questions for Understanding

- What are the cues you can use to know when to switch to a new dance step (after eight beats of music)?
- What are ways to remember the sequence of dance steps?

FREE MOVEMENT

Objective

To explore different movements to pieces of music using free movement

Specific Skill Focus

Dance

Equipment

CD player and a suitable music CD

Setup

Provide an open space for students to move.

How to Play

In terms of free movement, there are four major elements: time, space, force, and shape (table 7.1). The idea is to challenge the students to move to music using two contrasting movements with two, three, or four elements.

Free movement dances have no defined structure. Simply select appropriate music with a strong beat, and have the students enact the various steps in their own ways. In the African unit example, the first dance step is "16 beats of stomping like an elephant." Each dancer will have his own way of performing this stomp. The next 16 beats has dancers prowling like a lion; again each dancer will have his own way of prowling. Use dance to supplement a unit of geography or literature or another subject.

An African unit might include the following:

16 beats of stomping like an elephant

16 beats of a prowling lion

16 beats of a tree swaying in the jungle

16 beats of joyful jumping

Repeat

A firefighter unit might include the following:

16 beats of putting on boots, jacket, oxygen tank, and helmet

16 beats hopping up and down as the fire truck rushes to the fire

16 beats swaying side to side with the fire hose

16 beats climbing up a ladder

16 beats climbing down a ladder

16 beats swaying side to side with the fire hose

16 beats hopping up and down as the fire truck returns to the fire station

16 beats of taking off a helmet, oxygen tank, jacket, and boots

Repeat

Goldilocks and the three bears might include the following:

16 beats walking through the forest

16 beats eating big spoonfuls of porridge

16 beats sleeping

16 beats running on the spot with high knees through the forest

Repeat

Cinderella might include the following:

16 beats of mopping the floors in a house

16 beats gently bouncing in a carriage to the dance

16 beats dancing with the prince

16 beats running home on the spot with high knees

Variations

Adding dance to different educational units is an engaging way to help students remember the content. Try dancing to drops of water going through the water cycle (floating in the air, falling from the sky, bouncing around in a creek, leaving a water sprinkler, and floating in the air), or imitating other animals, or enacting other stories.

Questions for Understanding

- How do you know when to begin the first set of 16 beats and when to begin the next ones?
- Are there different ways to do the same dance challenges (e.g., different ways to stomp like an elephant)?
- How do you make sure you use both sides of the body equally?

MORE FORMALIZED DANCES

The previous section covers dances that are more open to personal development and exploration. There are also dances that have been choreographed, and it is fun, engaging, and physically demanding to try to repeat these dances as they have been developed by others. Three online examples are Ethno Tension, Don't Sit Still, and Move Your Body. They can be found by doing an online search under videos for "www.youtube.com/watch?v=5awIUNsaKD4" and "www.youtube.com/user/CIRAOntario/videos" In addition, use your computer browser under videos to search for "children fitness dances," and many other great examples will be displayed.

Three other examples are available through your purchase of this book. Go to the product page at www.HumanKinetics.com/products/all-products/Physical-Education-for-Homeschool-Classroom-and-Recreation-Settings to view the following dances: Eddie the Razor, Aerobic Routine, and Cumbia Urbana. These dances are also available on the book, DVD-ROM, and CD resource *Everybody Move! A Multimedia Package for Daily Physical Activity*. Any song with a strong eight-beat rhythm will also work. We have created three cue sheets to help you learn and perform these dances.

Cue Sheet
for Aerobic Routine

March sequence
Squats and lunges
Grapevine: 4 times
Grapevine with gluteal kick: 4 times
V-step right: 2 times
V-step left: 2 times
CHORUS
Knee pump, right side: 8 times
Step touch: 8 times
Knee pump, left side: 8 times
Step touch: 8 times
Alternating knees: 4 up, 4 back
Power squats: 4 times
Pulling weeds: 4 up, 4 back
Power squats: 4 times
Heel chugs
CHORUS
Shuffle right
Lunge behind: 4 times
Shuffle left
Lunge behind: 4 times
Step-touch sequence

Reprinted, by permission, from CIRA Ontario, 2010, *Everybody move!: A multimedia package for daily physical activity*, 2nd ed. (Champaign, IL: Human Kinetics).

Cue Sheet
for Eddie the Razor

Shoulder shrugs: 8 times

Attitude

Point to the foot: 16 times

Funky fish: 8 times

Ophea hand jive

Power lunges: 16 times

Jumping jacks: 8 times

Heel chugs: 16 times

Point to the foot: 16 times

Funky fish: 8 times

Ophea hand jive

Power lunges: 16 times

Jumping jacks: 8 times

Reprinted, by permission, from CIRA Ontario, 2010, *Everybody move!: A multimedia package for daily physical activity*, 2nd ed. (Champaign, IL: Human Kinetics).

Cue Sheet
for Cumbia Urbana

Part 1

Funky Egyptian: 2 sets

Basic and side cumbia: 2 sets

Part 2

Backward crawl: 2 sets

Egyptian drag: 2 sets

Part 3

Circle stomp: 2 sets

Single dog lifts: 4 sets

Double dog lifts: 2 sets

Repeat part 1

Part 4

Bongo squat: 2 sets

Backward crawl: 2 sets

Repeat part 3

Repeat part 1

Repeat part 2

Funky Egyptian: 1 set

GYMNASTICS

Play is the highest form of research.

Albert Einstein

Historically, gymnastics has been considered an Olympic sport that involves the performance of sequences of physical movements requiring physical strength, flexibility, and kinesthetic awareness. Today, gymnastics has expanded to include many types, such as general gymnastics, rhythmic gymnastics, sport aerobics, trampoline, synchronized trampoline, circus gymnastics, and educational gymnastics. This chapter focuses on educational gymnastics.

Educational gymnastics revolves around the development of movement skills in four themes, namely body awareness, space awareness, effort, and relationships. Educational gymnastics with educational games and dance is collectively part of the overall movement education approach to teaching physical education, a method of teaching originally developed by Rudolf Laban in the mid-nineteenth century. It concentrates on teaching children about their bodies in ways that encourage exploration so that they understand what the body can do (body awareness); where the body moves in space (space awareness); how the body can move (effort); and what relationships the body has with objects, other players, and itself. Instead of focusing on specific stunts, as in Olympic gymnastics, educational gymnastics is more child centered and a natural progression of the exploration of fundamental movement skills.

Exploration and discovery allow children to progress at their own pace and thus to experience more success in movement development (Pica 2004). Further, educational gymnastics parallels the philosophies of Teaching Games for Understanding because it is centered around creating questions for the students to answer through movement so they more fully understand what they are doing. For instance, when a first-grade teacher wants to teach her students the skill of rolling, she will ask a question to help them explore their own understanding of how their bodies can roll, such as "How many different ways can you roll along the mat?" rather than just saying, "Do a forward roll." Table 8.1 provides a helpful overview of the four movement themes and subcategories that movement educators use to guide their students through the discovery of these themes.

The following sections describe the main fundamental skills in gymnastics. After each skill description is a list of sample questions you can ask your students as they are developing to help them explore and understand the movement themes. In addition, this chapter provides suggestions for progression and sample lesson plans.

SKILL DEVELOPMENT FOR FIRST TO FIFTH GRADES

Five skills—rolling, transference of weight, balance, climbing, and hanging and swinging—are developmentally appropriate for children

Table 8.1 Movement Concepts

Body awareness *Actions of the body*	Space awareness *Where the body* *moves*	Effort *How the body* *moves*	Relationships *With what or whom* *the body moves*

Body shapes
• Curved
• Twisted
• Narrow
• Wide
• Symmetrical
• Asymmetrical
Nonlocomotor
• Swing
• Sway
• Twist
• Turn
• Bend/curl
• Stretch
• Sink
• Push
• Pull
• Shake
Locomotor
• Walk
• Hop
• Jump
• Slide
• Gallop
• Skip
	Location
	• General space
	• Self-space
	Directions
	• Up/down
	• Forward/backward
	• Right/left
	• Clockwise/counter-
	  clockwise
	Levels
	• Low
	• Middle, medium
	• High
	Pathways
	• Straight
	• Curved
	• Zigzag
	Extensions
	• Large/small
	• Near/far
		Speed, time
		• Fast
		• Slow
		Force
		• Strong
		• Light
		Flow
		• Bound
		• Free
			Objects or others
			• Over/under
			• On/off
			• Near/far
			• In front of/behind/
			  beside
			• Around/through
			Partners/small
			groups
			• Leading/following
			• Meeting/parting
			• Matching/mirroring

Reprinted, by permission, from J. Rink, T. Hall, and L. Williams, 2010, *Schoolwide physical activity: A comprehensive guide to designing and conducting programs* (Champaign, IL: Human Kinetics), 63.

of preschool and primary school age and can safely introduce them to the experiences characteristic of traditional gymnastics (Pica 2004). Note that mats or carpets should be used when rolling and transferring weight.

Rolling

Rolling is a horizontal transference of weight that can be done different ways. In kindergarten, children should be asked to explore ways they can roll their bodies, perhaps in different shapes, such as a pin shape (log roll). The forward and backward roll is considered a more advanced skill and does not have to be performed perfectly at this level. Rather, begin by asking children to roll in different shapes as well as different directions, such as backward and forward.

Questions for Understanding

- How many different ways can you roll along the mat?
- Can you roll along the mat in a stretch shape? What about a curled shape?
- How many different directions can you roll along the mat?
- Can you roll along the mat using your upper torso to start the action?
- Can you roll along the mat using your lower torso to start the action?
- Can you roll along the mat in a tight ball position?
- Can you roll along the mat with your hands tucked into your chest, not letting your hands touch the mat?

Transference of Weight

Transference of weight is a smooth shift of weight from body parts to body parts. Locomotion, such as walking, is considered weight transfer because you are moving your weight from foot to foot. However, transference of weight can also take place without locomotion, such as when moving from a sitting to a lying position on a mat or shifting the body weight from the hands to the feet (Pica 2004). You can assign students certain body parts to begin with and to end with. Next, have them rock and roll on different body parts and see how the weight moves from one body part to the other (the questions for understanding give good examples of this progression). Rocking and rolling on different body parts is a great progression into another balance. Also, you can progress their movements by encouraging them to transfer quickly and more smoothly.

Questions for Understanding

- How many different ways can you transfer your body from one end of the mat to the other?
- Can you transfer your weight from your knees to your hands?
- Can you transfer your weight from your knees to one side of your body?
- Can you transfer your weight from your bottom to your back?
- How can you transfer your body from your hands to your elbows?
- How can you transfer your body from your elbows to your back?
- Can you transfer your body from the top part of your tummy to the bottom part of your tummy?
- Can you transition without stopping?
- What did you have to do to transition without stopping?
- What do you have to do to make your body move more quickly through each transfer?

As children reach third to fifth grade, they will become interested in other skills such as the cartwheel and roundoff, which are advanced transferences of weight. There are different kinds of cartwheels, but in general a cartwheel is a transfer of weight sideways, performed by starting in a standing position, bringing the hands to the ground while the body inverts and the legs travel over the body, and then coming back down to a standing position one leg at a time. The roundoff is similar to the cartwheel except you land on both feet at the same time, and there is more momentum used throughout the action. The following gives tips to help in teaching.

- **Cartwheel.** An effective method of teaching children how to do a cartwheel is to place them in groups of three with a jump rope. Have two children in each group stretch out the jump rope and hold the ends about knee high. The other child will try the cartwheel by placing her hands on a mat or soft ground space and attempting to kick her legs over the jump rope. A demonstration works well. The children holding the rope can increase the height of the rope over time to get the child doing the cartwheel to kick her legs higher. Another idea is to stack some mats; each child stands on the mats, slowly places his hands on the ground, and then kicks his feet off the mats to the ground. This is good for those having trouble landing the cartwheel because it gives their feet another second to rotate under them to allow them to land properly. Supervise this activity to make sure the children do not overrotate.

- **Roundoff.** The first step with a roundoff is to learn to kick up. Draw a small circle or use tape at the center of a mat; you can put numbers on the circle like a clock. Ask the students to place their feet at 6 o'clock and their hands at 12 o'clock and kick up. They should work on getting their hands and feet together. For more details, please refer to the websites and resources appendix.

Balance

A player is balanced when her center of gravity is over a small or narrow base of support, such as one foot, two hands, or the hand and elbow. Two feet is considered a narrow base of support if the feet are close together, but two feet is easier than other bases of support, so encourage the children to progress from there. Balance is a good skill to do after transference of weight because the children can naturally transfer their weight from a position they hold into another position they hold. As mentioned previously, they can do this easily after learning to rock and roll.

Balances can be static or dynamic. Static is when the position is held still, and dynamic is when the position is held in a moving action, such as walking on a balance beam (Pica 2004). You can have students hold their bodies in a still position on the mats and then explore a walking balance on a line you have made on the floor. For progression, you can challenge them to move sideways and backward on the line (Pica 2004).

Questions for Understanding

- Can you hold your body still on three different body parts?
- Can you hold your body on three other body parts?
- What did you have to do with your center of gravity in order to hold your body still in a balance?
- Can you try to balance your body on two body parts other than the feet?
- What did you have to do to balance your body on two body parts?
- Can you balance your body and then transfer your weight to a different balance?
- Can you start with a balance, transfer your weight, and then end in another balance?
- Can you do this without stopping?
- What did you have to do to keep the movement flowing smoothly?

Climbing

Climbing is a skill that involves "pushing and pulling and supporting one's weight while moving the body up and down" (Becka 1993, p. 6). Climbing is essential because it helps children develop overall body strength and stamina. Use any apparatus that allows them to climb on and off, such as the equipment in a park (Pica 2004). You can have pre-kindergarten-age children practice getting on and off furniture and then progress to higher items. Try to create a space for children to explore. You can also play imagination games by pretending that what they are climbing is something else, like a mountain, tree, or ladder (Pica 2004).

Questions for Understanding

- What body parts are you using to pull yourself up the "mountain"?
- What body parts are you using to push yourself onto the "mountain?"
- What do you find easier, pushing or pulling?
- What do you have to do with your legs when you are pulling with your arms?
- What do you have to do with your arms when you are pushing with your legs?
- Can you pull and push at the same time?

- What happens when you push more with your legs?
- What happens when you pull more with your arms?

Hanging and Swinging

Hanging and swinging are great skills for developing upper-body strength. It is recommended that children hang from an apparatus no higher than their heads, and the arms should be straight (Pica 2004). Once they learn to hang with their arms and lift their legs, the swinging action will come naturally. As far as activities to play, you can count their swings. Start with one and continue to challenge them. If there is more than one child, you can do a collective count altogether, so even if a child swings once, she is still contributing to the overall count. When children are on swings, watch that they do not swing too high, and make sure you are supervising them.

Questions for Understanding
- What are your hands doing to keep your body off the ground?
- What do you have to do to keep your grip on the apparatus?
- What do you have to do to start swinging your body?
- Is it better to bend your elbows or to keep your arms straight?
- What do you do with your body to keep yourself hanging longer?

OTHER TYPES OF GYMNASTICS

Some types of gymnastics are too dangerous to attempt with young children, unless a trained professional is teaching and spotters are available. For instance, apparatuses found in advanced gymnastics, such as the vault, box horse, balance beam, and uneven bars, have been taken out of the physical education curriculum because of accidents that have occurred. However, children would benefit from incorporating some other types of gymnastics into the educational gymnastics program. Rhythmic gymnastics, trampoline, sport aerobics, some circus forms, and general gymnastics can add excellent variety. Children in third to fifth grade in particular enjoy using props such as ropes and ribbons, jumping on trampolines, and trying to jump and use props while being synchronized. Rhythmic gymnastics is especially fun and is very effective when doing the theme of relationships and learning to manipulate objects such as ribbons, balls, and hoops. You can explore more ideas in the resources at the end of the book, or visit local gymnastics and dance schools in your area.

PROGRESSION

With respect to progression through table 8.1, body awareness is a beginner concept, followed by space, effort, and relationships. All four can be introduced to kindergarten-age children (e.g., exploring the use of different body parts). In first grade, students should demonstrate an understanding of the basic skills in educational gymnastics, including the use of different body parts, types of effort, space, and relationships. They can also start to work with partners, if possible. In second and third grade, they should be able to select and perform the basic skills in educational gymnastics and then develop a sequence, which involves putting one or more skills together and practicing them so they flow fluently. In fourth grade, students can work on refining the basic skills in educational gymnastics, practice performing sequences, and work in bigger groups. Group work or collaboration that focuses on synchronizing, copying, matching, and mirroring is very important in children's development (Lathrop and Murray 2002). Finally, in fifth grade, children can apply and refine basic skills and elements of body and space awareness, effort, and relationships and combine them to form more challenging gymnastics sequences individually, with a partner, or in a group.

USING THE MOVEMENT THEMES AND VARIATIONS

Any of the lessons in this chapter can be used as a base, and you can vary them with different focuses. For instance, if you want to teach acceleration and deceleration, you can incorporate these skills in any of the lessons by asking the children to run fast throughout the mats and then slow down when they get to a mat in order to control their bodies throughout the transference of weight. Once you have tried one lesson, you will find it much easier, and you will see how the flow progresses the students through tasks. It is also easy, once you are comfortable, to use the chart (table 8.1) to incorporate other themes in your lesson to progress the children's skill levels. In addition, you can use props and variations of types of gymnastics in these lesson plans. For example, you can add balls, hoops, or ribbons during the movement development part of the lessons and then have students use the props in their sequences. The older children really like using the props in partner and group routines. You can even have the props all in a pile and ask them to choose what they want to use. Have fun with it. You will be so impressed with what the children come up with.

LESSON FORMAT

A lesson on gymnastics should last anywhere from 30 to 60 minutes. Start with a warm-up, usually 5 to 10 minutes, depending on the time you have. In the warm-up, get the children active while also introducing them to the movement themes. Then in the second part of the lesson, progress to movement development, where you work on developing their skills. This part will last approximately 10 to 20 minutes. Last is performance, or sequence development, which should take up the greatest amount of time, approximately 15 to 30 minutes. It is good for the upper ages to have enough time to prepare and show their sequences.

ROLLING SKILLS

Objective

To have students develop body awareness through exploring different body parts and transferring their weight

Specific Skill Focus

Rolling

Equipment

Mat for each child if possible or a soft surface

Setup

Gather in an open space in your home or outside on the grass. Scatter the mats throughout the space, with enough space in between for the children to get through as they run.

Warm-Up (5 to 10 minutes)

Ask the children to run through the space without touching the mats and while avoiding each other. After a few minutes, ask them to change directions. The young children will need more instruction with respect to changing directions. Look at the chart under space to see what directions you might want to teach them. When they are back in the forward-moving position after a few minutes, instruct them that when they get to a mat they are to roll along the mat anyway they want. Children in third to fifth grade might have an idea what rolling is, but first and second graders might need you to show them what you mean. Show them the log roll and forward roll to start. Have them go from mat to mat for a few minutes.

Movement Development (20 minutes)

Have each child find a mat. Ask the children to explore different ways of rolling on their mats. You will see the children explore how to roll in their own ways at first. For the first graders, you need to let them have fun and explore what they can do on their own. It is interesting to watch the children being creative as they learn to use their bodies in different ways along the mat.

After a few minutes, see if they can get their bodies in ball shape (like an orange) and roll, and then in long stretched shape (like a hotdog) and roll. Once children can manipulate their body parts long and stretched to perform a log roll, ask them to try initiating the rolls with first the upper torso and then the lower torso. Teach them to tuck their heads and go slowly.

Once children reach second grade and until fifth grade, they will need to advance and demonstrate their rolling skills. For a forward roll, you can look for the following to help them do the rolls correctly:

- Are they standing with their legs apart?
- Are they placing their hands on the mat near their feet? (The closer to the feet the better.)
- Are they looking through their legs until they see the ceiling?
- When they see the ceiling, are they pushing with their toes? (To prevent the top of the head from hitting the mat.)
- Do they feel the back of the head touch the mat? (If they feel the top of the head touch, they need to look more for the ceiling and push more with their toes.)

For a backward roll, the children can start from a squat position and rock themselves backward until the palms of their hands are both on the mat. To keep themselves round, you can ask them to keep their knees tight to their chest. For progression, you can move from a flat mat to an incline mat for both a forward and backward roll (Pica 2004).

You can use the questions for understanding at this point. For instance, as they are exploring on their own on the mat you can ask, "How many different ways can you roll along the mat?" or "Can you roll along the mat using your lower torso to start the action?"

NOTE: A more advanced activity for third to fifth grade is "footsie rolls," where pairs of children lie on their backs with the soles of their feet together and then attempt to roll without their feet breaking contact (Pica 2004). Another fun roll is egg rolls, where they kneel with arms crossed and resting on the mat, knees pulled into the chest, and head tucked. The children then roll sideways in both directions, keeping the head tucked (Pica 2004).

Progression

You can use this same lesson plan and add elements for progression by looking at the chart and changing minor things. For instance, explore body shapes and directions more; or start getting into themes of effort, where they run fast and slow down when they get to a mat in order to learn to control their body weight before they roll.

Culminating Activity (20 minutes)

Children can start learning to do routines at any age. The younger children will have more trouble with this, but you can help them. The idea is to let them explore creating a routine where they go from one roll to another, back and forth along the mat without stopping. You are trying to progress them into transferring their weight from one roll to the other. Help them try one roll along the mat and then either try a backward roll or turn around and do a different roll. Just start slowly and see how they do. Some older children will be able to explore and create routines on their own. For third to fifth grade, it is a good idea to have them do this in pairs. Have them show their sequences to each other, either in groups of children at the same time or individually.

TRANSFERENCE OF WEIGHT

Objective

For children to understand what it feels like and what it means to transfer weight from one body part to another

Specific Skill Focus

Weight transfer

Equipment

Mat for each child if possible or a soft surface

Setup

Scatter a mat for each student throughout the space.

Warm-Up (5 to 10 minutes)

Tell the students to run around the space, and every minute or two say, "Freeze." Ask them to run on the spot for a few seconds and then keep going. The next time when you say "Freeze," tell them to take a step to the right and then a step to the left and then keep going. Ask the class, "What are you doing when you step from foot to foot?" (Answer: "You are transferring your weight from foot to foot.") Ask them other questions, such as "Can you transfer your weight from the heel to the toe?"

Movement Development (20 minutes)

Ask all the children to each get on their own mats. Here the children will explore different ways of transferring the weight of their bodies. A good way to learn about transference of weight is rocking and rolling actions. Ask them to rock their bodies, first slowly and then faster. Then you can progress them to see that if they rock fast enough they will eventually roll. The rolling is a transference of weight.

Incorporate questions for understanding here. For instance, you can explore more questions, such as "How many different ways can you transfer your body from one end of the mat to the other?" or "Can you transfer your weight from your knees to your hands?" As they explore, you can move through the questions for understanding provided or make up your own questions. As the students become capable of doing the tasks, continue to progress them. Watch to see how they are doing, and help them as you feel necessary.

NOTE: After the students have explored on their own mats for about 10 minutes, you can ask more questions for understanding to help them progress, such as "What different body shapes can you do with your body on the mat?" Then ask them, "Can you hold the shape for 10 seconds?" Then ask, "Can you hold your shape and then transfer your body [weight] out of the shape into another shape?" For this task, watch to see that they are trying to go from shape to shape without stopping and holding the shape.

Progression

The first graders will explore the basic tasks longer and will not be able to progress. After about 10 minutes of exploration, you can teach specific skills such as hopping, jumping, cartwheels, and roundoffs, all of which are transferences of weight and require different skill levels. The younger children can learn how to hop, the difference between hopping and jumping, and how these skills are transferences of weight. The older children can progress into cartwheels and roundoffs. Review the description of cartwheels and roundoffs to see how to teach the children the progression.

Third graders to fifth graders can progress from here into different body parts leading an action. This teaches them to fluidly move their bodies from shape to shape through their transferences of weight. You can help them explore their body parts by asking, "When you are in a curled shape, can you slowly get into a stretched shape with your hands and feet leading?" Show them how to do this. Ask the students more questions, such as "Can you lead a transference of weight using another body part, such as your head?" Get them to explore different ways of leading their transferences of weight with different body parts leading the action.

Culminating Activity (20 minutes)

Finally, tell them to create a sequence. The younger children will do this alone with your help, and the older children will work well in groups of two or four. Give them direction about what has to be in the sequence based on how the children progressed during the movement development. For instance, they might need to include three different shapes and three different transferences of weight. This is an example of a sequence where these movements flow together. Let them explore, help them if they need it, and have them show their sequences to each other.

BALANCING BODIES

Objective

To teach children body awareness through balancing their bodies on different body parts as well as to develop a foundation for developing bone and muscle strength

Specific Skill Focus

Balance

Equipment

Mat for each child if possible or a soft surface

Setup

Scatter the mats around a large space.

Warm-Up (5 to 10 minutes)

With the students running throughout the space, freeze the action every 30 seconds or so. The first time you say, "Freeze," tell them to stand on one foot and balance themselves for a few seconds and then keep going. The next time, tell them to explore different ways to hold their bodies in a freeze position. Then on your call, they continue to run throughout the space until you call freeze again. After repeating this for a couple of minutes, have them run throughout the space, and when they get to a mat, they are to transfer their weight along the mat and then continue running until they get to another mat. You can progress them through this by getting them to hold a body position when they get to a mat, then transfer their weight, then transfer along the mat, and then hold a body position at the other end of the mat.

Movement Development (20 minutes)

Ask the children to find their own mats, and then ask some questions about balance, such as "What does it mean to bear your own weight?" (Answer: "It means you are supporting the weight of your body"). Next say, "On your mat, try to bear your weight on four body parts." Show the students what you mean. For the younger children you can give the example of a dog standing on four legs. Instruct them to try four different body parts and then another four different body parts. Continue to progress them by incorporating the questions for understanding, such as "Can you bear your weight on three body parts?" "Can you bear your weight on two body parts?"

NOTE: At some point you will need to explain to the children that bearing their weight on only two body parts means they are bearing the weight of their bodies on a small base of support. When we take our body weight on a small base of support, we call that a balance.

Progression

Help the children with their balancing skills by getting them to stand and try to balance on different body parts. Teach them that lowering their bodies will help them with their balance because it lowers their center of gravity, which brings everything closer together. "Everyone stand. How can we improve our ability to balance?" (Answer: "Increase your base of support and lower your center of gravity.") Ask them questions to help them understand what a balance is, such as "Are you balancing when you are standing on two feet that are placed wide apart?" (Answer: "No, because the majority of your weight is not supported with a small base of support.") Have the children explore standing balances and balances on their mats. After about 10 minutes, ask them to try balancing and then transferring their weight out of that balance and into another balance. The older children would be ready to try a headstand at this point. Check the resources for the progression of a headstand and how to transfer out of this skill.

Culminating Activity (20 minutes)

Ask the students to develop sequences with three balances and three transferences of weight in between. The younger children can do this on their own, and the older children can form groups of two or more. For the older children, fifth grade in particular, it would be fun for them to learn counterbalances so they have more fun with the sequences, such as a wheelbarrow, leapfrogs, or Chinese sit-ups (where they are sitting back to back and then try to stand up).

REFERENCES AND RESOURCES

CHAPTER 1

American Academy of Pediatrics. (2007). The Importance of Play in Promoting Healthy Child Development and Maintaining Strong Parent–Child Bonds. http://pediatrics.aappublications.org/content/119/1/182.full.

Bunker, D., & Thorpe, R. (1982). A model for the teaching of games in secondary schools. Bulletin of Physical Education, 18(1), 5-8.

Butler, J., and Griffin, L. (2010). *More Teaching Games for Understanding: Moving Globally*. Champaign, IL: Human Kinetics.

Canadian Sport for Life. www.canadiansportforlife.ca.

United Nations Human Rights. (n.d.). Convention on the Rights of the Child. www.ohchr.org/EN/ProfessionalInterest/Pages/CRC.aspx.

Werner, P., Thorpe, R., and Bunker, D. (1996). Teaching games for understanding: Evolution of a model. *Journal of Physical Education Recreation and Dance, 67* (1), 28-33.

CHAPTER 2

Fitness Testing Website

Centers for Disease Control and Prevention body mass index (BMI) calculator: http://apps.nccd.cdc.gov/dnpabmi.

Equipment Suppliers

Gopher Sport offers high-quality products and services: www.gophersport.com.
Bender Balls can be found at www.benderball.com/store.php.

Warm-Up, Cool-Down, and Stretching Websites

Public Health Agency of Canada: www.phac-aspc.gc.ca/pau-uap/paguide/child_youth.

Their free downloadable resources include the following:

- Family Guide to Physical Activity for Children
- Teacher's Guide to Physical Activity for Children

- *Gotta Move!* interactive magazine for children
- Physical activity chart and activity stickers

Wikipedia. Dynamic Stretching. http://en.wikipedia.org/wiki/Dynamic_ stretching.

Youthwork Practice. Games With Clothespins. www.youthwork-practice. com/games/clothespins-games.html.

YouTube. Dynamic Stretching. www.youtube.com/watch?v= DkCZym9CT54.

Additional Materials

Alter, M. (2004). *The Science of Flexibility*. Champaign, IL: Human Kinetics.

Byl, J. (2004). *101 Fun Warm-Up and Cool-Down Games*. Champaign, IL: Human Kinetics.

Flexibility for Sport and Fitness. (1997). Videocassette. Champaign, IL: Human Kinetics.

Kurz, T. (1994). *Stretching Scientifically: A Guide to Flexibility Training*. 3rd Edition. Island Pond, VT: Stadion.

Stretching and Flexibility. (1997). Poster set. Champaign, IL: Human Kinetics.

Teaching Flexibility. (1997). Videocassette. Champaign, IL: Human Kinetics.

Testing Your Flexibility. (1997). Poster. Champaign, IL: Human Kinetics.

CHAPTER 3

Bowling

Jowdy, J. (2009). *Bowling eXecution*. 2nd Edition. Champaign, IL: Human Kinetics.

Mullen, M. (2004). *Bowling Fundamentals*. Champaign, IL: Human Kinetics.

Website

For world records with plastic discs:
World Flying Disc Federation. WFDF World Records. www.wfdf.org/ history-stats/world-records.

CHAPTER 4

Basketball

American Sport Education Program. (2012). *Coaching Youth Basketball.* 5th Edition. Champaign, IL: Human Kinetics.

Paye, B., and Paye, P. (2013). *Youth Basketball Drills.* 2nd Edition. Champaign, IL: Human Kinetics.

Disc

Parinella, J., and Zaslow, E. (2004). *Ultimate Techniques and Tactics.* Champaign, IL: Human Kinetics.

Football

American Sport Education Program. (2010). *Coaching Youth Football.* 5th Edition. Champaign, IL: Human Kinetics.

Colby, G. (2013). *Football: Steps to Success.* Champaign, IL: Human Kinetics.

Lacrosse

American Sport Education Program. (2003). *Coaching Youth Lacrosse.* 2nd Edition. Champaign, IL: Human Kinetics.

Soccer

American Sport Education Program. (2011). *Coaching Youth Soccer.* 5th Edition. Champaign, IL: Human Kinetics.

Luxbacher, J. (2013). *Soccer: Steps to Success.* 4th Edition. Champaign, IL: Human Kinetics.

CHAPTER 5

Badminton

Grice, T. (2008). *Badminton: Steps to Success.* 2nd Edition. Champaign, IL: Human Kinetics.

Tennis

Brown, J., and Soulier, C. (2013). *Tennis: Steps to Success.* 4th Edition. Champaign, IL: Human Kinetics.

Volleyball

American Sport Education Program. (2007). *Coaching Youth Volleyball*. 4th Edition. Champaign, IL: Human Kinetics.

Kenny, B., and Gregory, C. (2006). *Volleyball: Steps to Success*. Champaign, IL: Human Kinetics.

CHAPTER 6

For world records in disc tossing:
World Flying Disc Federation. WFDF World Records. www.wfdf.org/history-stats/world-records.

For 12 more disc games go to:
Team Makers. Disc Games for Kids. www.teammakers.com/overview.aspx.

Baseball

Benson, R., and Benson, T. (2010). *Survival Guide for Coaching Youth Softball*. Champaign, IL: Human Kinetics.

Keller, D. (2011). *Survival Guide for Coaching Youth Baseball*. Champaign, IL: Human Kinetics.

CHAPTER 7

CIRA Ontario. (2010). *Everybody Move!: A Multimedia Package for Daily Physical Activity*. Second Edition. Champaign, IL: Human Kinetics.

Everybody Move! features a teacher guide with fitness activities, music activities, and line dance descriptions; a music CD; and a DVD-ROM with dance video clips and breakdowns of routines. With this resource, you can get your students moving and having fun, regardless of your expertise or your limitations on space or equipment.

CHAPTER 8

Becka, D. (1993). Educational gymnastics: Recommendations for elementary physical education. *Teaching Elementary Physical Education, 4* (1-6).

Lathrop, A., & Murray, N.R. (2002). Collaborative learning in educational gymnastics: Strategies for success. *Physical & Health Education Journal, 68* (2).

Pica, R. (2004). *Experiences in Movement: Birth to Age 8*. 3rd Edition. Clifton Park, NY: Thomson Learning.

Websites

Department of Education for the Province of British Columbia: http://www.bced.gov.bc.ca/irp/welcome.php.

Helpful website with learning outcomes, instructional and assessment strategies, and a list of learning resources.

eHow: www.ehow.com/video_2346608_do-forward-rolls-beginner-gymnastics.html.

Helpful video on forward rolls. If you let it keep running, the instructors will lead you through other rolls, cartwheels, handstands, and other gymnastics elements.

Books

Mitchell, D., Lopez, R., & Davis B. (2002). *Teaching FUNdamental Gymnastics Skills*. Champaign, IL: Human Kinetics.

Ortiz, K. (2013). *Tumbling Basics*. Champaign, IL: Human Kinetics.

Werner, P., Williams, L.H., & Hall, T.J. (2012). *Teaching Children Gymnastics*. 3rd Edition. Champaign, IL: Human Kinetics.

ABOUT THE
AUTHORS

John Byl, PhD, is a professor of physical education at Redeemer University College in Ancaster, Ontario, Canada, where he teaches wellness courses. Byl is president of CIRA Ontario, which promotes fun active participation for all through intramurals and recreation programs. Byl is a member of the Christian Society for Kinesiology and Leisure Studies (CSKLS) and is the host of their listserv.

Byl has been a professor since 1986 and has edited, authored, or coauthored over 20 books, including *Physical Education, Sports, and Wellness: Looking to God as We Look at Ourselves.* He is a recipient of the CSKLS Presidential Award, which recognizes those who have displayed actions compatible with the mission of the CSKLS. In 2013, Byl was awarded the Queen Elizabeth II Diamond Jubilee Medal for his significant contribution to making physical activity a priority in his community and in the country.

Bettie VanGils Kloet is certified as a fitness professional and has been working in the fitness industry since 1996. She helps many clients reach their fitness goals through her business Fit4Life With Bettie. Her teaching focuses on fun, form, and fitness goals. She holds a bachelor's degree in French from UWO as well as a teaching degree from Redeemer University College. Bettie home-schooled her children for 10 years and now encourages other families as a homeschool conference speaker. She lives in Hamilton with her husband and three children and enjoys reading, cross-country skiing, cycling, canoeing, and spending time with family and friends. She volunteers as a Sunday school teacher and a youth ministry leader in her church, and she is a proud member of the Velodonnas, a women's recreational cycling group.